MW00623421

ARMOR YOUR MIND

MASTER MENTAL RESILIENCE IN THE FACE OF
ADVERSITY & CONQUER YOUR AMBITIONS WITH
CONFIDENCE

CARL PROX

WWW.ARMORYOURMIND.COM

ACCOLADES
PUBLISHING LLC

Paperback ISBN: 978-1-7379363-0-5

Ebook ISBN: 978-1-7379363-1-2

Hardcover ISBN: 978-1-7379363-2-9

CONTENTS

DEDICATION

To my beloved wife,

Daria Prox

You are the most selfless, caring, and hard-working woman in all of existence. Who you are inspires me to be better in every aspect. I am beyond blessed to share this life with you as your husband. I love you with all my heart!

Accept Your **FREE Gift**, a Copy of **THE RULE OF 8!**

You are about to be one step closer to a healthier, happier, more fulfilled you!

In just a minute, you'll be able to access your FREE copy of **The Rule of 8**, a guide that will help you achieve the work/life balance you've always wanted.

Learn how to get the most out of a 24 hour day by managing your time in the most efficient way possible. After spending **years** feeling frazzled, burnt out, and unfulfilled, you can now maximize your health, sense of contentment, and even productivity by following the instructions in this simple, easy to read ebook.

Visit the link below to get a free PDF of **The Rule of 8** and start following it **today**!

WWW.THERULEOF8GUIDE.COM

INTRODUCTION

"Life doesn't get easier or more forgiving; we get stronger and more resilient."

— STEVE MARABOLI

Here's the one fact that everyone knows — life is hard.

It's full of problems, setbacks, crises, challenges, and everyday ups and downs. The funny thing is, if it wasn't like that, we wouldn't be talking about life at all, but about a blissful slumber that never requires us to get out of bed. Let's face it — that isn't living and we don't have that option, thankfully.

I imagine that you know how it feels to be down, unable to get up and go on. You may be physically exhausted, mentally fatigued, or emotionally drained. You could have been dealt one of life's hard knocks and feel wounded, traumatized, or scared. It may be that your confidence is at rock bottom and your self-esteem is non-existent. Stress, anxiety, and even depression could have taken over as the dominant forces in your world. Negativity and a sense of helplessness may be keeping you in a very dark place.

It can be so, so difficult to get out of these cycles, especially when you really just want to throw in the towel, give up, sit down and cry, or worse.

I know how that feels because I've been there.

Growing up, I had to deal with a lot of issues, and they had an extremely negative effect on my self-confidence. Talking to you about it now is easy, but that wasn't always the case. A few years ago, I couldn't even have a conversation with myself about how I was feeling, never mind with someone else. Everything was just stuck inside my head and I really couldn't deal with a lot of the problems I was facing, let alone confront what I had experienced when I was younger.

For as long as I can remember, there had been turmoil in my life, beginning when I was around four years old with my mom's severe depression. Any one of you who has been in that position knows how scary it is to see one of your parents turning into a ghost before your very eyes. By the time I was seven, she had developed schizophrenia, which made her very erratic and unpredictable. I often didn't know what state I would find her in when going home from school, but I do have one particular recollection of her drinking an excessive amount of wine one night, and then becoming extremely aggressive and paranoid.

My dad wasn't around that much due to his work, and I often felt very insecure, not knowing what tomorrow would bring. That insecurity was compounded during my early school years as a victim of bullying and I developed a terrible stutter around that time. My schoolwork suffered as a result, and if you had a similar experience while at school, you would know only too well how being a "special ed" kid can leave its stigma on the psyche. Feeling that you are "stupid" does absolutely nothing for your self-confidence, and you even begin to believe that it is true after a while.

Looking back, I can rationalize it all and sympathize with myself, but that feeling of hopelessness and low self-esteem had a profound effect on me while growing up. There are some things that I found very difficult to talk about for many years, and one of those was the fact that I was also sexually abused by a family member when I was 10 to 11 years old. Anxiety, shame, and guilt became my middle names, and these were issues which I dealt with alone as I grew older. Before that time, I was living in the mountains with my family and happily enjoying the outdoor life. I loved climbing trees and exploring nature, something which I still get a lot of enjoyment from, thankfully.

Luckily for me, I found an outlet in wrestling at school thanks to my friend Anthony, who introduced me to the sport. This led me to meeting my wrestling coach, Stan; and if it hadn't been for him, I don't know where I would have ended up in life. The chances are that I would have ended up becoming involved in petty crime, joining a gang, or worse. By the time I got to senior year in 2008, the market crashed and my family lost everything, forcing us to move. However, I was determined to stay on at school until wrestling season was over. So, when my family members finally left, I stayed behind.

The next few months were spent couch-surfing at friends' houses and I even had to sleep on the street a few times. Luckily, the parent of a good friend of mine named Julio was kind enough to open up his home to me, and I lived with them until the wrestling season finished. Possibly, during that period, I got a small taste of what it means to believe in yourself and to make decisions based on that, as well as seeing what the consequences of that could be. I always had my dad as a good role model and knew that he had sacrificed spending a lot of time with his family to earn a living, so maybe in some way that gave me the courage to go on.

One thing I NEVER thought would be of any help to me was reading a self-help book. So, when I did begin looking into it, I've got to tell you that I was completely over-whelmed by the number of books out there on self-confidence, resilience, mental strength, and so on. You've probably read quite a few of them yourself and may have, like me, concluded that many of them say the same things but in different ways.

It's definitely not my intention in this book to reinvent the wheel. What I can do, though, is bring you some sound advice and practical help based on my in-depth research on the subjects of mental resilience and emotional well-being. I've examined what highly qualified experts have to say on the topics, from prominent psychologists to influential life-coaches, and I've explored hundreds of different mind techniques that we can all use. You could say that I've fished in the lake and caught all the big fish.

As a mentor, I have been fortunate enough to share what I learned with a wide range of people and help them to work through whatever was holding them back from reaching their goals and feeling fulfilled. Now, I want to share those techniques with you so that you can also feel empowered to handle whatever life throws at you and come out of it stronger, happier, and more resilient.

They say that whatever doesn't kill you only makes you stronger. I guess that's just another way of saying that negative experiences are character-forming. I don't subscribe to that view, because I would never wish for anyone to undergo trauma, emotional pain, or mental stress in the first place. What I have learned is that under-going a difficult time or event doesn't necessarily make you a better person — it can have the opposite effect and cause real damage to your well-being. But life is like that;

it often deals us cards we weren't expecting and demands that we play the game anyway.

What is more important to me is being able to cultivate a self-protective shield that can help us to channel our potential into something more positive, which is why I have named this book **Armor Your Mind.** But before you get the wrong idea, it's not about being tough, uncaring, hard, or unfeeling. It is actually quite the opposite!

This book is about building your own mental armor that will not only offer you protection from external "threats" in the world around you, but, more importantly, strengthen the inner you: your central core. It's a bit like one of those toy transformer characters in a way, because as you learn more about how to develop positivity and self-confidence, you will be transforming yourself from within.

By working through each chapter, you will begin to assemble a full suit of armor that will shield you from your own negative thoughts and help you to build up your mental resilience in the face of adversity.

We all have the ability to cope with life's problems; and what we don't know, we can learn. That's the beauty of resilience — it is a mental skill that can be taught, nurtured, and developed. As you go through the book, you will also discover why even vulnerability is a strength that can help you to move on in your life. You will find out how practicing tunnel-vision focus will enable you to achieve your goals and ambitions. Hopefully, by the time you reach the end of the book, you will have mastered the art of mental toughness and emotional resilience, without feeling the need to sacrifice the things that are important to you.

You can transform into the person that you want to be, equipped with the tools that you need to handle anything in life and the mind armor to protect you.

It's not going to be easy.

Growing a different kind of mindset is hard and may even seem impossible for some of you. That's because you have become so used to that negative cycle in which your mind keeps telling you what to do, what to think, and what to feel. And take it from me: your mind is not always your best friend — it can often be your worst enemy.

Start by viewing this book as your safe space. No one here is going to judge you, criticize you, or make you feel like a failure. This is a place for inner reflection, self-compassion, and hope. I'm here to tell you that whatever it is you have gone through in the past or are facing in the present, you can build yourself a full set of armor for your mind. It will show you how strong you really are and provide you with clear strategies to help you grow and get rid of any self-doubt.

Upon reading this book, you will become a skilled craftsman of your own life, equipped with the tools you need to be a survivor and not a victim. It will teach you how to deal with stress, anxiety, or depression, and liberate yourself from that sense of despair. By discovering how negative thinking works, you will be able to regain control of your own happiness. It will also help you to banish those feelings of "not being good enough" or "too weak" and get you to focus on what is important. Finally, in this book, you will unlock the secrets to building mental resilience while remaining compassionate and sensitive to your own needs, as well as the needs of those around you.

I started out on this journey just like you: looking for something that would make me feel better about myself and my life. I used to think I was a tough guy who had gone through a lot and yet, had come out of it kind-of OK. But deep down inside, I knew that I wasn't handling things well at all. If I could avoid facing my emotions, I would, and I listened far too much to the constant negative chatter going on in my head instead. It was like turning the music up to full volume in order to drown out the silence, because that would be too scary to even think about.

Then, something happened. The noise became too loud — things in my life took a nosedive and I realized that I needed help.

In 2019, my wife was admitted to the hospital for emergency treatment. She was 21 weeks pregnant with our first child but was suffering from severe preeclampsia, which causes extremely high blood pressure and organ failure. It can be life-threatening for both mother and baby. After a few days, the doctors told me that I had to make a choice between my unborn son and my wife's life.

I was screaming inside, and my own voice was terrifying me. I asked God why he was making me choose... I didn't want to have to choose... I didn't want to have to make the choice between one or the other! How could I do that when I loved them both equally? That sense of rage and the burden of the responsibility hit me like a gigantic tidal wave. But I knew there was no one else in this world who could make that decision but me.

As we held tiny Elijah Alexander and looked at his perfectly formed little nose, hands, and feet, we knew that we had to say goodbye to him eventually.

It's funny how life is one big circle. One minute, I was the kid who needed protection, and the next, I'm the guy who is protecting his family in any way he can. I think that experience brought me to my senses — call it a revelation if you like. I began to see more clearly just how strong I am, and how I can also have a positive effect on others. I believe now that I always was resilient — I just didn't know it and nobody was there to tell me so.

Everything that I experienced when I was younger had an effect on me, from my low self-esteem to my stutter, including being deeply in debt on leaving high school. They were my ways of coping then. Not great, I admit, but as humans, we find incredible ways to deal with all of the hard knocks that life throws at us. Sometimes, that means suffering inside, and it can also result in hurting those around us. The truth is that everything I went through was in the past, and I got to the point where I needed to put it behind me and look forward to a brighter future.

I didn't want to live with the noise anymore.

I needed to sit with myself and just listen to what the inner me had to say. That was when I faced the truth of the real me: who I am, and who I want to become. It then felt like a door had opened for me and I could begin to see a bright future worth fighting for.

What I really needed was a strategy that I could apply to my own story — something effective and hands-on that I could implement. At that point, the best thing I could think of was to start reading, researching, and studying everything that the experts had to say about resilience and self-confidence. I searched high and low for theories, techniques, opinions, and recommendations, picking up anything useful I could find on my way. After some time and countless hours of introspection, I gradually began to see how all the pieces fit together.

That's when I realized that I needed to channel my strengths and make them work for me. I understood how I had been allowing my mind to run rampant, giving it far too much freedom until it was wearing me down. It became clear that by training my thoughts and getting rid of negative self-talk, I could create a stronger, more posi- tive me; and it worked. Now, my mind is my ally, not my enemy, and I use it to help me deal with any hurdles, obstacles, and challenges that come my way.

You can do it too. All you need is a little bit of trust in yourself and the desire to get out of that negative mindset. However unsettling it may seem, a willingness to get out of your comfort zone can turn your life around for the better. If you are tired of feeling down on yourself and stuck in a hopeless cycle, there is a way out. It is possible to reach for your goals and lead a fulfilling life, and this is the place to start. By working through each chapter, you will acquire all the pieces you need to build yourself a full suit of armor for your mind and finally start to enjoy life with confidence and positivity.

Life really can be more fulfilling, rewarding, and bring you greater joy. It all begins here, so let's get started on that mind armor!

1

ARMOR PIECE 1 — POSITIVE THINKING

There are some phrases people use that really have no impact whatsoever.

How many times have you been told to *cheer up, think positive, look on the bright side?* Although the person telling you this may have your best interests at heart, it doesn't mean anything if you are feeling broken and totally disillusioned with life. No amount of rosy pep talk is going to make you feel any better.

You see, no matter what people say, if you don't believe enough that things can and will get better, they may as well be talking to a brick wall. In fact, someone telling you to "be positive" when you have just gone through some kind of trauma or dramatic, life-changing event is not the kind of thing you want to hear.

So, while kind words are acceptable, they are not enough. If you want to improve any aspect of your life and change your perspective on your potential for happiness, the idea of being positive has to come from within. It is a thought process that you must adopt, and it is the first piece of armor that is going to strengthen your resolve and resilience.

Our thoughts are our artillery in a way. They are what we use to get through every second of our day. They are pretty powerful tools and if we use them well, the sky's the limit. But if we let them control our every move, then we are surrendering to their will. It's quite simple really, and there is also plenty of research to back up what I am saying — your thoughts can either make or break you!

Imagine that you have two friends who are both training for an upcoming wrestling tournament; let's call them Jarrett and Liam. Jarrett has worked a lot to prepare for the match and is eager to step into the circle to prove just how skilled he is. He believes that he will win and doesn't entertain the possibility of losing. He is full of positive energy.

Liam, on the other hand, has also trained equally hard to make sure he is prepared to meet his opponents. Nonetheless, he is dreading the tournament and believes he is going to lose. He keeps telling himself that he is not good enough, and dreads stepping onto the mat. He is full of negative energy.

Here's the thing: who do you think is more likely to do well in the tournament — Jarrett or Liam? I would place my money on Jarrett because he is going in there with a winner's mindset. Even if he loses, because of his positivity, he isn't going to mope around and feel like a failure. He will think about what he did wrong, try to correct it, and start getting ready for the next opponent. Liam, on the other hand, will be absolutely miserable if he fails, and will probably find it very hard to deal with losing. If he wins, great; but he won't necessarily feel that his success was due to his hard work. He may even put it down to being a twist of fate, or just good luck.

People who think positively never beat themselves up when things don't go their way. They learn from their mistakes and prepare to take on the next challenge in life. This is the kind of thinking that most successful people have, and there's plenty of evidence to support that. People who think negatively tend to experience failure more often and will not try as hard to achieve their goals. But don't take my word for it. This isn't just some double-talk or feel-good theory. It is based on countless in-depth studies that have been taking place for years, and the more we learn about the way our brain works, the more we can understand the power of positive thinking.

WHAT DO THE EXPERTS SAY?

A successful life

We used to think that successful people must be happy people. Now, thanks to studies such as the one featured in the *Psychological Bulletin* (December 2005), we can say that it's happiness that makes you successful, rather than the other way around. What the researchers found was that people who feel happy attribute their success to their optimism and positivity. After examining the responses of over 275,000 people in the study, the head researcher, Dr. S. Lyubomirsky of the University of California, Riverside, concluded that when people feel happy they tend to feel more confident and optimistic. As a result, others find them to be likable and sociable, which can lead to even greater success.

A healthy life

But being positive isn't only useful in terms of success in life. It has also been shown to have a significant impact on your health. Usually, if you are facing a crisis situation for a short period of time, the adrenaline burst that you get is actually a boost to your immune system. We need adrenaline to spur us into a fight-flight-freeze response and it's therefore working in our favor. But if you are in a place where you just can't see the light at the end of the tunnel and this goes on and on for an extended period, this can have severe repercussions on your body. A study by Dr. S. Segerstrom at the University of Kentucky in 2009 showed that this war of attrition on your immune system inevitably leads to medical conditions such as frequent illnesses, depression, anxiety disorders, and worse. It is better for your health to think positively, even when you are going through a hard time.

A longer life

The healthier you are, the more chance you have of living a longer life. When researchers at the University of Kentucky looked at the longevity enjoyed by nuns living in the same convent for over thirty years, they came to some astounding conclusions. The *Nun Study*, as it is called, involved examining the autobiographies of nuns, ages 18-32, written in 1930. The entries were rated on a scale of positivity. When the researchers contacted the nuns who were still alive 60 years later, half of them had lived beyond the average life expectancy, and all of them had scored highly on positive thoughts or feelings in their journals. Now you know one of the secrets to a long life!

A coping mechanism

Positive thinking can also help you to cope in times of great stress, which is why it is now being taught to soldiers in the U.S. Army as a preventative measure for PTSD. The *Penn Resilience Program*, which is based on decades of research, teaches people to become more resilient to stress and anxiety by increasing their levels of positivity. This works as a coping mechanism when experiencing stress or trauma at work or school and strengthens their mental fitness. Anyone can benefit from it, even kids, and by learning from an early age how to manage stress, they can grow up with better mental resilience in all aspects of their lives.

A positive image

When we are worried about something, we imagine the worst outcome, which causes anxiety. In a 2016 study, researchers from King's College, London, examined 102 subjects who had been diagnosed with severe anxiety disorders. They asked one group to visualize an image of a positive outcome for something they were worried about, a second group to think of positive verbal outcomes, and the third group was asked to visualize any positive image whenever they started to worry. The results showed that the two groups that visualized a positive image reported decreased anxiety and greater happiness. The power of visualization is extremely potent, and we'll come back to that subject later on in the book.

I could write pages and pages about the research undertaken on the benefits of positive thinking, but I think you can get the message from the above examples. Not only do they show how positive thinking can bring you more success and deal with problems more effectively, but they also point to the health benefits and increased life expectancy that you can enjoy.

SO, WHAT EXACTLY IS POSITIVE THINKING?

Positive thinking is a mental attitude in which you expect good and favorable results. It's the process of creating optimistic thoughts, rather than pessimistic ones. A positive mind anticipates happiness, health, and a peaceful ending in any situation. Sounds easy? Well, it is a process that requires learning some skills, just like anything in life, and you have to be prepared to reboot your brain in order to make it work for you.

It isn't so much about how you feel because, quite often, those feelings are a direct result of your thought patterns. You may feel disheartened and sad about something that happened to you, but those feelings are created by what your brain is telling you to feel. And the longer you continue to feel like that, the more your brain will get used to following that pattern. So, you have to stop and take a good look at how you see life — a half-full glass or a half-empty one?

Some of the skills you will have to master if you want to switch to that positive-thinking mode are:

- Changing negative thoughts into positive thoughts
- Finding the positive aspects of the situation
- Stopping pessimistic thoughts from interfering
- Seeing the need for positive thinking
- Knowing how to manage large problems by dividing them up

- Establishing optimistic beliefs about each part of the problem
- Helping yourself to challenge pessimistic thoughts
- Placing positive feelings over negative thoughts

Only you can make this happen and, no matter what is going on around you, no one can get inside your head and do the necessary re-wiring. If you feel that it is going to be difficult, then you are right — it is. But think of it this way: if you aren't happy with your life, then it's up to you to change it. No one else is capable or maybe even willing to do that. This book is about helping you to have more mental resilience, but it has to start with your belief that you can succeed. That is your first step towards thinking positively and I know you can do it.

What I would like you to do is to put yourself first for a while. I don't mean that in a selfish or egotistical way. I just mean, take some time to be with yourself — to see what your "self" needs, and nurture a stronger, more optimistic you. You could think about things like:

- Self-encouragement
- When was the last time you gave yourself a pep talk about the positive qualities that you have?
- Self-assertiveness
- When was the last time you felt confident in any given situation?
- Self-instruction and purposeful thinking

- When was the last time that you drew up a plan and went about putting it into action?
- Self-affirmation
- When was the last time you thought, "I can do this"?

Can anyone adopt positive thinking?

I will be the first one to say that, yes, anyone can achieve it if they want to turn their life around and be happier, healthier, and more successful. Hey, who doesn't want that?

We are all looking for ways to enjoy life more and to fulfill our dreams or life goals. You may have had a tough life or are going through some difficult moments now. You could feel lost and full of self-doubt, even facing unprecedented difficulties that you don't feel prepared to cope with.

One of the things you need to know is that YOU ARE RESILIENT.

If you weren't, you wouldn't be here now. You can take more than you think, but it may not seem that way at the moment.

Another thing that I want you to grasp about positive thinking is that it doesn't mean sticking your head in the sand and hoping that everything will turn out wonderful. That is just naivety and running away from the real issues. You have to confront whatever it is you are facing, and if you do it armored with positive thoughts, you are halfway there.

I think that when we are young, especially in our childhood, we aren't really prepared for processing stress. We may experience it, but we aren't able to consciously deal with it in a way that can be managed and prevented from harming us. I remember at a very young age feeling very scared when my mom got sick. I couldn't understand then what was happening to her and, as a four-year-old, I just saw her disconnecting from the world. That's a very frightening thing for a child to witness and seeing her unwilling to talk, eat, or even get out of bed in the morning was like experiencing a great loss for me.

Back then, I couldn't process any of those feelings and certainly didn't have the emotional or mental maturity to understand what I was going through. As an adult, of course, I have a much greater understanding of how debilitating depression can be, and I now have the skills that allow me to deal with that. Children have a resourceful habit of burying things but, as adults, we need to keep everything visible and on the surface so that we can be in a better position to process them. If you are locked in a negative mindset, you won't be able to cope, no matter how old you are. But if you have a positive mindset, you will find a way through. Positive thinking isn't about having a sick relative and saying, "It'll be OK," and walking away. It won't be "OK," because that person needs help and support. You could have a sick child or a partner who is going through some emotional turmoil. It's not "OK" to ignore that. Neither is it "OK" to ignore your own pain or issues. You have to face those too.

Positive thinking is about living in the real world, with all its negative experiences, and being able to carry on without sacrificing your health and well-being. When it comes to health, there are benefits for both your physical and mental well-being, so don't consider positive thinking as just being about feeling "happy." It is much more profound than that.

Here's a checklist of some of the advantages to having that positive mindset:

1. Reduced risk of having a heart attack
2. Better overall physical health
3. Greater resistance to illness, like the common cold
4. Lower blood pressure
5. Better stress management
6. Improved pain tolerance
7. Longer life span
8. Less depression
9. Better coping skills
10. Better mood
11. Clearer thinking
12. Greater problem-solving skills
13. More creativity

You know how it feels when you are down, right? Being on the dark side of the moon can make you feel lethargic, exhausted, give you headaches, and a feeling of being unwell in general. Is that your imagination or is your body trying to tell you something? Research has shown that, amazingly enough, people who have a positive outlook are less likely to get sick and report fewer symptoms when exposed to the flu and common cold. In another study, it was found that women who were more optimistic were less likely to die from cancer, heart disease, stroke, respiratory disease, and infection. That's a very big deal! Research also supports that if you are optimistic about life, you are more likely to enjoy a healthy lifestyle, which is obviously beneficial for your long-term health.

There is a great deal of evidence available revealing that people who are more optimistic recover faster from illnesses and procedures such as coronary artery bypass surgery, while positive thinking has also been shown to help lower blood pressure and hence the chance of heart attacks. That makes a lot of sense if you think about it. Whenever we get stressed, our body goes into overdrive, with our blood pressure soaring. This may not be too bad when it happens occasionally, but when it keeps happening over a long period of time, it can be catastrophic. So, strategies for dealing with stress are a very important aspect of positive thinking.

We all get stuck in negative thought patterns from time to time, but learning to recognize this is the next step to avoiding it. Ask yourself in all honesty: Do you feel any benefits from thinking negatively? I am sure your answer is going to be no, but getting "unstuck" from that requires a bit of effort.

You can answer a few questions to see just how much of a negative thinker you are. Be honest, because acknowledging the truth is a positive step toward helping yourself:

1. Do you have negative thoughts about yourself, such as your appearance, capabilities, or achievements?
2. Do you feel that everyone is against you?
3. Do you hide things from others because they may criticize you?
4. Does the thought of change make you feel stressed?
5. Do you think that your best is never good enough?
6. Do you often feel unlucky, compared to others?
7. Do you often say, "I'm not good enough, smart enough, strong enough"?
8. Do you always see the worst-case scenario?

Even if you answer yes to just some of the above, it's not hard to see that your negativity may be sabotaging many aspects of your life. Usually, along with negativity, there are underlying factors such as low self-esteem and lack of self-confidence, which we will look at in the next chapter. The funny thing is, the longer you perpetuate the myth that it's all doom and gloom, the less likely you are to feel good about yourself. And so it goes on... being negative can bring negative outcomes, and leave you feeling that you don't have what it takes.

It's time to bust that myth once and for all.

If you ask any successful person how they view life, you can guarantee that they are going to give you a positive response. *Life is great, life is wonderful, and they feel capable of taking on anything.* You probably won't hear them worrying about if it's going to rain tomorrow or what their friends think of them. Being positive can make all the difference in how you view yourself and that positivity rubs off on others, making you great to be around. Think of it this way: How many people do you consciously go out of your way to avoid, because all they do is complain about this, that, or the other? On the other hand, how many people do you enjoy being around because they ooze positivity, confidence, and happiness?

When I talk about positive thinking, I'm really talking about the ways that we can adopt a more positive frame of mind and believe that when we think more positively, we feel better and can function better. It's quite a simple premise and doesn't need an in-depth knowledge of positive psychology, which is more scientific/study-based. Positive psychology covers a wide spectrum of expertise and generally focuses on behaviors that lead to a more optimized frame of mind, such as cognitive-behavioral therapy. The definition of positive psychology, as laid out by its pioneers Martin Seligman and Mihaly Csikszentmihalyi, is *"the scientific study of positive human functioning and flourishing on multiple levels that include the biological, personal, relational, institutional, cultural, and global dimensions of life."*

I'm not a doctor, psychologist, or therapist, and what I offer in **ARMOR YOUR MIND** is my own view of positive thinking based on my life experience and through helping others. If you feel that you have issues that require more specialized help, by all means, seek out that assistance. In the meantime, by reading this book, you may begin to unravel some of the problems that are holding you back from enjoying life to the fullest.

NEGATIVITY BIAS

To be fair, our brains are pretty much geared towards negativity — it's called **negativity bias** — and it's something that we have carried around with us since humans were created. Back in those days, we needed to pay attention to what was going on around us as a matter of life or death. If you were more attuned to the dangers, you had a much better chance of survival; hence, you were more likely to pass on those genes of focusing on the negatives rather than the positives. Make no doubt about it— the folks back then had to be aware of their environment because they knew full well that they could be attacked by predators at any minute. Their negative expectations were very logical and our brain continues to try to keep us safe, even though it is now overreacting most of the time to environmental cues.

How does this run over into negative thinking today? Well, it means that we continue to look on the downside rather than the up. In most of our interactions, we are much more likely to notice all of the negative aspects and even be able to recall them in great detail later on, while we are unable to remember the positive aspects. That's why traumatic experiences stay with us for so long, while we may forget any pleasant moments that we have experienced. I bet you can bring to mind in vivid detail something bad that happened to you — the time, the day, who was involved, what was said, and so on. But can you remember a pleasant experience that you had years ago in the same detail?

When you are a kid at school and told that you are stupid by the teacher, or even by your parents, those words stick with you for much longer than someone telling you, "You did good buddy." Anything negative that you experienced has been ingrained in your memory, and you probably play that event over and over again. I get you.

In a way, we still tend to respond based on some kind of hardwired instinct, but it doesn't have to be like that. Just because our brain has this bad habit, it doesn't mean that we can't change it. When someone makes a comment that you find insulting, there is no need to keep ruminating over their words all day. Neither is it necessary to report that you had a terrible day when you get home, based solely on that one negative comment. Your day may have been great, but all of that fades into insignificance in the light of a few mean words. You can change that reaction; and you should, because it isn't something that serves you or makes you feel good about yourself.

Negativity bias can bring us down, so it's essential to be aware of that and look for ways to catch it before it escalates. Imagine, for example, that you have an argument with your partner. Afterward, instead of dwelling on what was said and how mean your partner is, think about their good points and all of the reasons why you are with them. Why make a drama out of a minor incident? Another example could be something embarrassing you recently did in public, like spilling your coffee over your friend. Instead of beating yourself up about how clumsy you are, just forget about it — your friend has probably done so already.

Your inner critic

There is a little voice inside your head that never shuts up. It is not your friend and does not have your best intentions at heart. It is the voice that keeps telling you what to do, how to think, and what to feel. Imagine a mean, toxic person who wants to sabotage your every move — that's your inner critic. We all have one, but we can reset the dialogue and make that inner voice our friend, not our foe. It all begins with how much freedom you give it to ruin your life. Telling yourself that you deserve to be mistreated, for whatever reason, is a negative pattern that you have gotten used to hearing. You have possibly created a scenario in your mind, based on a past experience, that you deserve the worst, and have stayed stuck in this dialogue, allowing your inner critic to repeat it over and over again. You have heard it so often that you actually believe it, which prevents you from feeling positive about yourself.

- This is the voice that magnifies the negatives and filters out the positives.
- This is the voice that personalizes everything, making you blame yourself in any given situation.
- This is the voice that turns everything into a catastrophe from the moment you wake up, just because you didn't hear your alarm.
- This is the voice that polarizes the world into good or bad, with no room for any middle ground. You are either perfect or a total failure.
- This is a harsh voice to live with, isn't it?

Positivity and resilience

So, what does all of this talk about positive thinking have to do with mental resilience? That's a good question.

Having a positive mindset doesn't mean that you deny reality, but it enables you to deal with life's challenges more efficiently and learn from them. If you are up for a promotion at work and don't get the position, having a positive outlook will prevent you from falling to pieces. It will also help you cope much better with the rejection and push you to work on your skills so that the next time a position comes up, you are better prepared to grab it. Positive thinking isn't a golden ticket to success by any means, but it is a way to go through life with optimism and form a greater "bounce-back" reflex.

Athletes have always known about the power of positive thinking. If they didn't, no one would ever compete in any sporting event. When you are going up against a faster or stronger opponent, it's your positive attitude that makes you compete, even if the odds are against you. An athlete is prepared to lose, even though he/she wants to win, and that's the kind of thinking that motivates him/her to succeed. We can all use a bit of the athlete's mindset in our lives, no matter what we are involved in.

Some of the traits that make positive people more resilient also include:

- Having faith in themselves and their abilities
- Expecting the best outcome and seeing setbacks as temporary
- Treating failures as an opportunity for learning
- Knowing their weaknesses and being prepared to develop their skills/knowledge

The way you respond to a setback plays a vital role in how you go on from there. If you react negatively, how are you going to find the motivation to try harder next time? When I was wrestling for my school, there were plenty of times when I experienced losses. Instead of moping around and telling myself I was a loser, I was determined to train harder, train for longer, and beat my next opponent. It was one of the most significant forms of structure in my life at that time, and it gave me something to focus on and eventually excel at. For you, it could be playing chess, or soccer — it doesn't matter what the activity is. The point is to keep trying, keep improving, and not to let a loss defeat you because that just isn't logical, is it? You may feel that you have failed at something else in your life — a relationship, for example. But having one failed relationship doesn't mean that you are destined to be alone for the rest of your life. It just means that this particular relationship wasn't meant to be, and it was time to move on. If you are optimistic about your future, you are much more likely to thrive than if you put your hands up in the air and say, "I give in."

Your mind is capable of doing amazing things, as long as you train it well. Humans can achieve the unbelievable but, on the way, they have to make a lot of mistakes. That's just the way it is — trial and error until you succeed. The most powerful weapon that you have is your mind, so fill it with positivity, not negativity, and you will see the results. I can promise you that!

HOW TO THINK POSITIVELY

Like I said earlier in this chapter, you need to do a little bit of re-wiring, but it can be done. Here are some simple steps to get you going in the right direction:

1. Stop the negative talk

When something happens, instead of listening to your inner critic, take control of the dialogue inside your head. So you didn't pass your driving test, or get that new job:

instead of fixating on what went wrong, consider what you learned from that experience and how you can prepare better in the future until you succeed.

2. Reframe your window

Going over and over your past mistakes means that you are reinforcing a negative view of what happened. Recalling those bad moments repeatedly is giving them so much power over you. When that happens, simply refocus and reframe — don't dwell on past negatives, as they won't do you any good. Instead, look for the positives and trust in yourself, giving equal weight to the good and the bad.

3. Get up and do something

It's easy to sit mulling over things that went wrong. But the more you do that, the worse you are going to feel. The next time you feel yourself sitting and thinking about past events, get up and do something active, like going for a walk or a drive. Cook your favorite meal or watch a movie. Just take your mind off toxic thoughts and enjoy doing something that gives you comfort instead.

4. Recall positive moments

Recall all the good things that have happened to you in your life and create space for them in your long-term memory. Remember how you felt when you last achieved something or had a great time and replay those moments repeatedly. After a while, that will become a habit and one that will leave you feeling optimistic about your future.

5. Imagine the best possible future

You can allow yourself to have the best possible future, no matter what your circumstances are now. Instead of being filled with desperation and hopelessness, create an image in your mind of what you hope for your future to be like. Make a list of your goals and ambitions and think about ways to make them a reality. The sun is already coming out from behind the clouds!

6. Focus on your strengths

This is one of the most important strategies that you can adopt. Write down a list of your strong points or qualities, such as being organized, kind, disciplined, patient, creative, or whatever. Once you have written them down, try to act on one of them every day. For example, if you listed one of your strengths as being kind, carry out a small act of kindness every day. This reaffirms your positives and, after a while, you won't even think about the negatives.

7. Identify your goals

It's easy to go through life without any goals but if you do so, how can you ever intentionally achieve anything? By thinking about what you want and how to get it, you have a plan to work towards, and that gives you optimism about your future. If you want to own a start-up, begin by making a plan for how you can go about it and identify any skills that you need to brush up on. Set your goals and then work towards them — one step at a time.

8. Laugh a lot

It is OK to laugh, even at yourself. Laughter is a wonderful therapy that increases your serotonin levels and makes you feel great. You can even practice smiling in the mirror and see how much better you feel when you do so. Seeing the humor in situations can be a great way to overcome challenges and reduce stress, so I highly recommend it.

9. Look after yourself

If you follow a healthy lifestyle, you are going to feel more positive, because exercise has an instant feel-good effect, and eating healthily aids your immune system. I know it seems more tempting to eat junk food when you have a busy schedule and to skip out on any kind of physical training, but in the long term, your health will suffer and this is an open invitation for feelings of low self-esteem to slip in. Don't do that to yourself.

10. Be with positive people

Positivity is contagious! When you surround yourself with positive people, you will notice how that positivity rubs off on you. Hanging out with negative people can increase your stress levels and doesn't offer you anything useful. Keep your distance from toxic people and seek out those who inspire you instead. Listen to their stories and ask them for advice or support if you need it. Positivity is something you can learn from others.

As I mentioned at the beginning of this chapter, our thoughts are our artillery and we use them to get through each day. When your mind is in a negative rut, your thoughts are going to follow, and that is like shooting yourself in the foot. Being mindful of how you think is the key to facing life with more positivity, which also gives you more control over your life.

This is the first piece of armor that you need to channel your resilience so you can be victorious through any adversity that comes your way. Once you begin to see the positives, you will start to see life through a new lens and become more fulfilled in every way. In the next chapter, we are going to look at self-confidence and I'll be giving you some useful strategies for how to build up your self-esteem.

I would like to leave you with a brilliant quote by none other than Bruce Lee, who said,

"Do not allow negative thoughts to enter your mind for they are weeds that strangle confidence."

— BRUCE LEE

I think that's a great thought to hold onto as we move to the next chapter.

2

ARMOR PIECE 2 — SELF-CONFIDENCE

D o you remember the guy in senior high who was on everyone's "favorite" list? The guy who had all the cute girlfriends, was a star athlete on the school football team and an "A" student? He seemed to be so full of self-confidence and nothing could hold him back from achieving whatever he set his mind to.

I'm sure that there were moments when you envied him and wished that you could be admired just as much. Those are the guys who we generally think of as having a big dose of self-confidence, the ones who will "get on" in the world. I've met many people like that in my time who seem to be very confident on the surface, but when you dig a bit deeper, you often find that their confidence is limited to specific situations or abilities. On top of that, there's also the question of how much self-esteem they have, which is something completely different from self-confidence.

It could be that the guy in senior high shone in many areas yet didn't have the confidence to disagree with his parents. So, when we talk about self-confidence, it's not as simple as we may initially think. It's pretty much agreed nowadays among experts that having self-confidence doesn't mean that you can function successfully in every given situation. While having confidence in yourself is a wonderful thing, it can only serve you fully when it's backed up by a deeper sense of self-worth.

HOW SELF-CONFIDENT ARE YOU?

If you look at it from that perspective, self-confidence is often overrated; it doesn't necessarily guarantee success in life, although it can play a vital role. If I ask you how much self-confidence you have on a scale of 1 to 5 (1 being none at all, and 5 being extremely self-confident), it's a good indicator of how you perceive yourself in general but doesn't reveal your real strengths and weaknesses.

You may feel quite self-confident about your physical abilities, and not so much about your intellectual ones, or vice versa. It could be that you feel super confident at work, and yet can't manage your personal relationships that well. Perhaps you exude self-confidence when it comes to DIY jobs around the house but have no confidence in dealing with your financial matters. You see, self-confidence is something that you may have in certain areas of your life and not in others, which is OK.

The point is to understand that having self-confidence is definitely a plus, but it's something that depends on a range of factors, many of which you can improve upon. If you are wondering how to define self-confidence, you could say that it's the belief in yourself and the trust in your abilities to meet everyday challenges and goals. I can even go further and say that having self-confidence brings greater happiness because when you feel sure of your abilities, you bring more success into your life. If you successfully materialize your goals, you are more motivated to work towards new ones, filling you with deep personal satisfaction every step of the way.

It's a good time to think about what aspects of your life you feel confident in, and which parts you believe are preventing you from reaching your full potential or making you suffer. You can make a list of the areas in which you feel most confident and the areas where you feel lacking. You could note, for instance, that you feel confident when it comes to your occupational skills, but not so confident when it comes to meeting new people. If your list is full of pluses and no minuses, that's great! If you can't think of any areas of your life that you feel confident about, that is fine too — that's why I'm here. I want you to know that you can increase your level of confidence in the areas that matter to you the most.

One thing that I want to stress is this: Self-confidence has more to do with how you see yourself than what you are really capable of.

Why? Because having self-confidence basically means that you feel secure about your abilities, qualities, and judgment. In other words, how much trust you have in yourself. It's **NOT** about how others see you, how many accolades you have on your wall, or how many friends you think you have. Self-confidence is much deeper than that — it's about the faith that you have in yourself.

WHY IS SELF-CONFIDENCE SO IMPORTANT?

By building up your self-confidence, you can experience:

- Greater self-worth
- More fun in life
- Freedom to act without second-guessing yourself
- Reduced feelings of anxiety and stress
- More energy and motivation
- Better interaction with others

As you can see from the above points, having self-confidence allows you to truly embrace life and all that it has to offer you. Not only does it make you feel good about yourself, but it also helps you to achieve more and form stronger relationships. That can bring an enormous sense of satisfaction and give real meaning to your life. Not only that, there has been plenty of research to show how important self-confidence is for your positive mental health, with various studies proving the link between feeling sure of your abilities and a healthy mindset.

What does a lack of self-confidence look like?

A lack of self-confidence can limit how happy you feel about your life, which is why it's important to get to the bottom of any negative impressions you have created about yourself. But how can we identify what it looks like when someone has a lack of self-confidence, or whether you suffer from this? Below, you will find some common traits and it is useful if you can think about how much you relate to them as you read them. Do you recognize yourself at all?

1. Feeling that you are unsure of yourself, even when dealing with a subject you are familiar with.
2. Avoiding difficult tasks because you fear that you may not pull them off successfully.
3. Over-worrying about mistakes you may have made for way longer than anyone else typically would.
4. Telling yourself that you aren't good enough — remember that negative inner critic from Chapter 1?
5. Having a sense that something is missing in your life and expecting other people or things to provide you with it.

6. Experiencing self-doubt and avoiding responsibilities or taking a particular stand.
7. Difficulty in expressing your views out of fear of being ridiculed or not taken seriously.
8. Unwilling to ask questions because you don't want to appear "stupid."
9. Avoiding any activity that requires you to speak in public or be put under the spotlight.
10. Failing to show initiative and preferring to follow instructions.
11. Not standing up for yourself when faced with criticism or opposition.
12. Avoiding any dialogue that may leave you feeling exposed.
13. Letting others take charge instead of assuming a leadership role.
14. Being unable to deal with people who are more assertive and dominant than you.

It's quite natural to relate to some of the above points. We all go through periods in our lives where our confidence may suffer as a result of something that happened to us. I can recall many occasions in the past when I felt deflated because things didn't work out my way, but the trick is to have a resilient mindset that helps you to get back on track.

I have personally been through all of the above while pursuing my wife, Daria. I would like to share with you the story of how we first met in 2012, and explain how we managed to overcome a few of the obstacles that stood in our way.

In 2011, I was taking part in a Christian mission trip called "The World Race." My team and I were supposed to be staying with a local ministry in the country of Moldova but, instead, our itinerary was changed overnight to the tiny breakaway state of Transnistria which borders Ukraine.

It was a long bus ride to our destination, and by the time we got there, my team and I were hungry and had slept very little. We were being hosted by Tiraspol Church at one of their locations, which used to be an orphanage. When I least expected it, we pulled up to the gate and there was Daria, standing with her friend and waiting to help my team settle in. It may sound crazy, but I knew there and then that she was going to be my wife: It was love at first sight.

As we were getting settled into our rooms, I asked her if she needed any help washing the dishes or gathering anything needed for my team. I started some small talk with her and hoped I would see her again after that day. About a week later, I saw her again at a church service and eventually asked her if she would like to get some lunch and maybe go for a walk, because I needed to tell her how I felt about her before it was too late. During our walk, we sat down on a bench in a park and it took every ounce of courage to share what was in my heart with her. I was terrified at the thought of rejection, but I knew I needed to try. After I told her how I felt, she replied that she had feelings for me too. We discussed the reality of the situation because we both knew that this was not going to be an easy journey as it meant having a long-distance relationship. However, our love for each other was strong and our faith was even stronger, which is what ultimately allowed us to go ahead.

It was extremely challenging and I was faced with many difficulties from that point onward. I had started and was operating my own business back home while trying to find opportunities to go back and visit her. It was very important for me to build up a relationship with Daria and to gain her family's trust. We were eventually wed in 2014 but spent the first year and a half of our marriage apart due to the USCIS losing our documents, which left us no choice but to start the process all over again. I was frustrated at every turn by red tape and the limitations that prevented us from being together. Initially, it was intimidating to have to deal with all of the visa requirements and paperwork, but we pushed through hurdle after hurdle and our perseverance and love for each other finally came to fruition. While pursuing each other, we had people telling us it would never work and personal struggles of self-doubt often came to the surface. There were many days where we laughed and cried with each other, but we were so in love and devoted to one another that nothing was going to stop us from being reunited again.

Eventually, we were able to get her visa processed, and in March of 2016, we were finally able to be a real married couple. Daria was able to join me in the United States and the icing on the cake was when she told me that she was pregnant with our son in 2019. I felt like the luckiest man alive!

Challenges like the ones I described above about my own personal story are part of life. It's all about taking a time-out to look at the situation, see what you can fix, and then continue on your path. It's definitely not about self-blame or self-criticism, both of which will only hold you back from reaching your goals. You have to believe that you can do it.

This may sound obvious, but the fact is that self-confidence comes from within you — from yourself. It's not something that you can buy or acquire through external means. If you want to feel more confident about your abilities and have more faith in yourself, you have to begin from within. Throughout **Armor Your Mind**, you will notice that most of what I am suggesting has to do with your inner self - your inner core. You can be inspired by others and encouraged on your way, and that's great. But if you aren't prepared to put the work in, you will falter after a while.

WHAT IS NOT SELF-CONFIDENCE?

I also want to mention what self-confidence **isn't**, because there is a lot of confusion surrounding that, which may make you feel like you are doing something wrong. I'm not talking about the loud guys who are full of themselves: the ones who talk everyone else down or act as if they are superior to you and me. You don't have to be a "know-it-all" to prove how confident you are — that's usually just a cover for someone who feels insecure.

Being over-confident has many pitfalls, so it's about finding the right balance. Imagine being led up Mount Everest by someone who claims to be an expert, while in reality, he has never climbed any mountain higher than 1,000 meters. That's the type of over-confidence that is just plain irresponsible. Even if he believes that he is capable, the reality is that his ego is way bigger than his actual abilities.

Being aware of your weaknesses is just as important as knowing your strengths, which is all part of the balance that I mentioned earlier. It's OK not to be good at everything — to have flaws and imperfections. In fact, it's completely human! What is imperative is that you are aware of them, because failing to see your weaknesses can lead you to make bad choices or decisions that could have a devastating impact on the lives of others, not just your own.

Believing that you are right all the time and refusing to listen to others borders on arrogance and makes those around you feel inferior. That's not a good way to treat people and, even if you are convinced that you are correct, you don't need to force your opinion on them. Some of the most confident people I have ever met tend to speak less and listen more. Making hot air doesn't gain you any respect or convince anyone that you are Einstein or LeBron James. Most folks can see through any exaggerations, and no one likes to be talked down to or bullied — something that overconfident people may have a bad habit of doing.

Although a lot of emphasis in the society we live in is placed on being self-confident, I also want to mention that there are some negatives to this push for us all to feel great about ourselves. It's interesting to note that, as we strive to be the best that we can be, there are a lot of unrealistic expectations placed on us by social media and the media in general. Many people seem to have tipped the balance in favor of narcissism, which is obviously not a positive or healthy trait to have. One recent study even made the correlation between the increase of self-confidence over the last 50 years and the rise of narcissism, so it's good to keep in mind that I am not suggesting such extreme forms of self-perception.

What about self-esteem?

Like I mentioned earlier, it may be the case that someone appears confident and yet still has very low self-esteem. That's because self-confidence and self-esteem are two different things. While you may feel quite good about your public speaking skills or your athletic abilities, it is possible that, inside, you have a very low opinion of yourself. That negativity usually stems from our childhood years and it is a lot trickier to overcome. The good news is that when you learn how to increase your levels of self-esteem, your confidence should also increase. It's not often that you find someone who has high self-esteem and low confidence.

A very successful doctor friend of mine has a huge, plush surgery practice in my hometown. As a neurologist, he had to work hard for many years to become qualified and gain experience in this highly specialized field of medicine. On entering his office, you can't help noticing all of his diplomas and certificates framing the walls, and each time I visit him, I am totally impressed.

One day, I made some kind of comment, like, "Your parents must be really proud of you and what you've accomplished." I was shocked at his response when he replied that his father still thinks of him as the kid who can't do anything right. He explained that no matter how many qualifications he amasses, deep down, he feels that he will never be able to earn his father's respect. That left me feeling very sad because this respected professional is still suffering from the low self-esteem created when he was a kid by his father.

Self-esteem is the same as self-worth and is all about how much we value ourselves. If you have a high opinion of yourself and feel good about who you are, then you have a healthy level of self-esteem, no matter what your circumstances. You can be very poor or even living on the streets and still have self-esteem. It's a core element of your mental and physical well-being and not only has a positive impact on how you feel but also helps you to overcome challenges and perform better in a work or home environment.

Why your self-esteem is important?

If you don't feel worthy, then who else will value you? That's not only a question well worth thinking about, but it is also key to human development. As humans, we have evolved with the need to have a positive view of ourselves, which satisfied our ability to form alliances with others and be part of a group. All of this ultimately led to better chances of our survival, since there is safety in numbers, so it's not surprising that we still crave social acceptance. Imagine if someone is low on self-esteem — who is going to want them in their group or team?

We all want to belong somewhere, and feeling excluded is not a nice position to be in. It can lead to a great sense of loneliness, which we know has been linked with depression and anxiety. So, the onus is on us to be likable, and that isn't going to happen if we don't even like ourselves. That's another reason why positive social feedback is so important to us, and why many people rely (unfortunately) on their social media popularity to feed their own positive self-view.

I guess I don't need to tell you that the greater your levels of self-esteem, the more chances you have of finding a partner and improving your social status, as well as simply feeling good about yourself. Imagine if your partner also has high self-esteem... all the research shows that as a personality trait, it's 50% hereditary, with the rest of our development relying on environmental factors. That's great news if you see your glass half-full, and not such great news if you see it as half-empty. But let's hope that you belong to the former category, right?

Instead of saying, "I was born this way," you can look at it from a different angle and appreciate just how much potential you have for self-development and growth. This is something that I firmly believe in. When your environment is positive and nurturing, that's a great help. When it isn't so supportive and caring, that isn't an excuse to feel sorry for yourself and quit. If you can tap into the intrinsic desire to be happy, you will strive even more to achieve your goals and eventually get used to reaping the rewards of that. All it takes is a shift in behavior and way of thinking.

Never forget the self-fulfilling prophecy: If you think you will fail, you probably will, due to self-sabotage. This reinforces your initial view that you will fail, while, if you believe that you can achieve your goals and purposefully go after them, you are more likely to succeed. This reinforces your view that you can succeed and, as a result, boosts your self-esteem even more!

HOW TO INCREASE YOUR SELF-CONFIDENCE

When it comes to mental toughness, confidence is high up on the list of attributes that will help you to build that armor and make you more resilient. Having the ability to adapt in the face of challenges and undergo less stress than others is a mark of resilience, and it can be learned by applying different strategies. If you believe that you are capable of solving a problem, you are already on your way to finding a solution and will be less likely to panic when things go wrong. In addition to that, by gaining self-confidence, the chances are that you will keep persevering until you get a positive outcome and won't give up at the first sign of difficulty. When you are in that mode, you are invariably more likely to succeed, which also increases your self-confidence.

My top self-confidence building strategies

Being self-confident isn't about faking it. You may have been in situations where you were extremely nervous and tried to hide that, but there are many tell-tale signs which can betray you. These signs can be evident in your body language, what you say, how you dress, and even what you tell yourself, so I'm not going to advise you to pretend because that is superficial. What you need to do is begin by believing in yourself — that is the fabric that holds your armor together.

There are many ways to have more faith in yourself and it all begins with the perception that you have of yourself. It's not connected to anything outside of that. Sure, someone can pay you a compliment and you feel great for the rest of the day but what happens when someone insults you? Are you going to let that ruin your day? No! Believing that you have worth, value, and mental strength has got to start with you, and acquiring self-confidence is a part of that.

Here are some strategies that you can use to reinforce your self-image, while also creating the right kind of impression that you want to convey to the world. By applying these strategies, you will see the results, and they will become life-changing habits that you'll wonder what you ever did without.

1. Correct your body language

It's a simple fact that when you look confident, you feel confident and even if it seems difficult at first, there are ways to practice improving your body language. Try all of these tips at home as often as you like, until they begin to feel natural.

Stand up straight. You'll never see a soldier at the position of attention with hunched shoulders, so correct your posture and stand up straight. This exudes more confidence than you can ever imagine. Check yourself when you feel you may be slouching and simply put those shoulders back and lift that head high.

See eye to eye. Look the other person straight in the eye when talking to them. Anything else just makes you look evasive, unsure, and maybe even untrustworthy. Eye contact also shows that you are interested in what the other person is saying, but watch that you don't glare at them continuously, which can be intimidating. About 60% eye contact is good for any given interaction.

Stay focused. Fidgeting during a conversation is very distracting for the other person and is a clear sign that you are nervous. If you can't avoid it, try to keep it to a minimum and practice sitting with your hands relaxed on your lap. You can do this wherever you are and will soon see how calm it makes you feel.

Take it slow. Flapping your arms around and walking too fast gives the impression that you are irritable, which does not convey confidence. Slow things down by counting at a regular, slow pace in your head and allow your body to move to that rhythm.

Shake hands like you mean it. Handshaking signifies that you come in peace and are glad to meet the other person, so adopt a firm (not tight) grip. You can practice this by shaking your own hand until you understand exactly which grip feels firm and steady.

2. Communicate with confidence

What you say and how you say it tells a lot about you. Sometimes, our lack of confidence really shows when it comes to talking, but don't be put off. There are ways to overcome this and gradually build up your self-confidence. Think about the following and see what you need to work on — practice makes perfect.

Be clear. Say what you want to say and don't mince your words. If you wish to say no, then say no. You don't have to defend your answers or justify your position with lengthy explanations. A clear "no" is understood by all.

Keep it short. When you embark on a conversation, don't begin it by explaining in minute detail where you are coming from. That sets the tone for a conversation in which you appear insecure about yourself. And when it comes to your opinion on a specific matter, simply state what you believe, without feeling the need that you have to justify your position.

Stick with what you believe. Someone with self-confidence doesn't crack at the first sign of opposition and join the other side. Adhere to what you believe in and stay true to your values and opinions — they are important.

Show interest. Ask questions to show you have been following what the other person said and convey a genuine interest in them. This is the action of someone who is not afraid to be vulnerable or admit that they don't know everything and creates better relationships with others.

Express with respect. You may not agree with the other person, but addressing them with respect shows that you don't feel intimidated or threatened by differing viewpoints because you are self-assured about your own.

Speak slowly. Gushing and rambling do not convey confidence and will make the listener confused or worse. Also, be mindful of words such as maybe, just, and perhaps, because they all show self-doubt or hesitation.

3. Make a SWOT analysis

This is a great way to learn more about yourself and to help you evaluate your goals and ambitions.

SWOT is an acronym for Strengths, Weaknesses, Opportunities, and Threats and is a useful exercise that you can do to help you clarify your thoughts and identify your goals.

You can do this easily by drawing four boxes on a sheet of paper. The first box has the heading STRENGTHS, the second one WEAKNESSES, the third OPPORTUNITIES, and the fourth has the title THREATS.

In the first box, simply write down what you believe your strengths to be. It could be anything, from skills that come naturally to you to things you have learned, or your talents.

In the second box, WEAKNESSES, look at some things that you are not happy with about yourself and write them down. You could include things like bad habits, negative traits, lack of certain skills, or recent failures.

In the third box, OPPORTUNITIES, look at external factors that you could utilize to your advantage. You can consider things like people you know, courses to help you up-skill, social events, or the feasibility of positive changes.

In the last box, THREATS, think of things that may prevent you from achieving your goals. You can write down possible obstacles that you will meet on the way, practical challenges, and factors such as money or living arrangements.

4. Stop comparing yourself to others

You will never be the same as someone else because you are unique. No matter how much you compare and contrast, trying to be like somebody else or judging yourself by their standards will NEVER make you feel happy. The only critic you need in your life is YOU!

- Set yourself as your benchmark and live according to YOUR values, opinions, and dreams. There is no better way to acquire self-confidence and self-esteem.

- Instead of looking at the achievements of others and feeling down on yourself, celebrate your own achievements, no matter how small.
- Reward yourself when you reach a milestone, even if it is a small one. Managing to go to the gym is a big deal when you would have rather stayed in bed. Give yourself a pat on the back for doing so.
- Don't expect yourself to be perfect. No one is, believe me!
- Stop assuming that everyone is having a better time than you, or is happier, richer, more successful, or even luckier. It's not important what other people are doing. What you are doing for yourself is all that matters.
- When you fail, be kind to yourself. Have self-compassion and don't linger on what you didn't achieve in comparison to anyone else. Even top athletes stumble and fall, but they get right back up again and keep on running.
- Challenge your assumptions about yourself. Forget what others may think of you and focus on your qualities, achievements, and aspirations. You are all that matters.
- Find a mentor if you are interested in being inspired by someone who will genuinely be able to help you. A mentor can guide you and nurture your positive qualities, as well as offer you good advice when you need it.

One thing I have learned over the years is that when I want to achieve something, focusing on others' achievements makes me doubt my own ability to pull it off. This was mental torture in a way and now, instead, I have learned to use situational awareness to channel my focus on my goal. Instead of saying, "What if...," I set about making a plan for action to get me to where I want to go. This kind of tunnel-vision focus helps me to keep my eye on the prize and not be distracted by uncertainty and self-doubt. It doesn't guarantee me success, but it gives me the momentum to work towards a goal. Preparing for failure is also a great strategy because, by taking into account any setbacks or hurdles I may face on the way, I can take measures early on to overcome them.

If you fail, take it as a lesson, because that is exactly what it is. It is NEVER the end of the world. You just have to be more prepared next time, try harder, and be aware of what can sabotage your plans. If you have been putting off doing something because of self-doubt, now is the time to stop comparing yourself to others and to follow your dreams. I know that you have the strength and willpower to make it happen!

5. Discover the power of faith

For me, faith is very important and my personal belief in God has steered me through many difficult moments. Without my faith, I don't know if I would be here now. It's my faith that has helped me to keep going when times became hard, and it continues to fill me with hope and optimism. You may have your own beliefs and live by them to the best of your ability, and that's alright. We can all agree to not judge one another merely by our spiritual walk in life but to build unity in the face of diversity. For me, God created us to be the salt and light of the earth, not gritty, dark ashes. Life is to be lived according to His will, not that of other people's, and self-esteem is rooted in the love He has for us.

- You can use faith to develop your confidence because living according to God's plan will help you to see how much worth you have as a person. Instead of being influenced by the opinions of others, put your trust in God, who always sees your true value. By all means, listen to different viewpoints, but don't let those words define you because opinions change over time, while God's love remains steadfast.
- Remember that when you have faith, nothing is impossible. The restrictions that you place on yourself are man-made and when you are in that negative place, you can't achieve anything. Trusting in God has allowed me to open up to the belief that anything is possible, and I have seen that manifest itself in many aspects of my life.
- No matter what you have been through or what emotional scars you carry around, having faith will counteract all of the pain. It isn't God's plan for you to suffer so stop giving power to all of the

hurtful experiences in your life and embrace joy and love instead. You deserve it!

- As a Christian, I believe that we are not perfect, but can be saved by God's Grace. No matter how often you fail or stray from the path, God's love is always with you and self-compassion is paramount. Being hard on yourself is destructive and doesn't reflect God's true purpose for you. You are human and God loves you for who you are, so learning self-acceptance can give you the courage to go on. If you practice self-compassion, you will begin to be more optimistic about life and open yourself up to the possibility of achieving your dreams. Being filled with self-loathing, on the other hand, will get you nowhere.

- It is up to you to change your perceptions about life and being positive has many benefits for your overall well-being. After all, the way you view things can have a massive impact on how you deal with any given situation. Negativity breeds negativity and inaction, while having a positive outlook encourages action and success. Weathering the storm with a belief that the sun will shine in the end is based on my faith in the scriptures and the love of Jesus. I never feel that I walk alone.

- Instead of complaining about small, insignificant things, see the bigger picture. Count your blessings and be thankful for this wonderful gift of life that we have been given. No matter how hard things may be for you, it is important to remember that those who savor the simple things in life experience greater happiness, despite a lack of money or material possessions. Time well spent with loved ones in God's presence is more valuable than anything else in the world, and I give thanks for that every day.

As we come to the end of this chapter, it is a good idea to reflect on your feelings of self-worth. How you view yourself defines all of the good or bad feelings that you experience. By changing that mindset, you can begin to acquire greater self-confidence, which will propel you towards success and well-being. I hope that the strategies I have laid out above will help you to do that. They are all attainable, once you decide to implement them, and don't require anything other than your commitment to improving your life.

When you master self-confidence, you will earn the second piece of armor that you need to be more resilient, which will allow you to achieve whatever it is you want. You will develop new habits that equip you with the tools to pursue your goals and lead a more fulfilling life. We are going to explore habits in the next chapter and look at strategies for stopping bad ones and cultivating healthier ways of being.

I can't think of a better way to finish than with a famous quote by Aristotle, an ancient piece of wisdom that still applies today. He said,

"We are what we repeatedly do. Excellence, then, is not an act, but a habit."

— ARISTOTLE

Let's find out exactly how you can apply that to your advantage in the next chapter!

3

ARMOR PIECE 3 — HABITS

From the beginning of my current deployment, I was communicating with my wife frequently; but after a few months, it began to get harder and harder to talk to her. It was as if the distance between us made talking to her too painful. FaceTiming just reminded me of how much I wanted to be home with her rather than having to continue my deployment and I struggled with that. I am sure that anyone who is involved in a long-distance relationship will understand exactly how I felt, and it's certainly something that many soldiers will be able to relate to.

So, after a while, I developed this bad habit of not communicating with her, and this went on for several months. What I didn't realize was how much I was hurting her in the process, and it was only when she cried out to me that I understood what effect my behavior was having on her. She had begun to think that I didn't care about her or love her anymore, which wasn't true at all. I was simply undergoing pain of my own because I had never wanted to be away from my wife for this long. We had done long-distance in our early years but for some reason, this situation was different.

After she shared her feelings with me about this, I quickly realized how selfish I was being. I wasn't considering how she must have felt or what was going through her mind as I continued not to communicate with her. After that, I started to call her regularly; not because I wanted to pass the time or out of habit, but because I love and care for her.

I did feel bad when I thought about what I had put my wife through and realized that there are so many examples of things that we unconsciously do in life without paying any attention to their effects. The above example is a good one because there are probably millions of people going about their lives not paying much attention to how their actions affect their loved ones. If you think about it, a lot of our behavior is habitual and, by its very nature, receives little or no attention from us whatsoever — it just happens. So how can we change what we don't like and build more effective habits that will help us to reach our goals and be more mentally resilient without causing upset to others?

One thing is for sure: Bad habits bring about bad results, while good habits bring more positivity and happiness into our lives. When it comes to developing patterns of behavior that serve us rather than harm us, there is a lot we can do to achieve that. Adopting good habits is an essential piece of armor that you need if you want to build up more mental resilience and you'll find out exactly why below.

If you remember the quote by Aristotle at the end of the previous chapter, we are what we do; so if we want to be better at anything and improve how we feel about ourselves, we need to acquire more self-enriching habits. But what exactly are habits and why do we develop them in the first place? Once we have gone through that, we will look at why having good habits is so important, and I'll give you some strategies that you can begin using today to acquire them.

WHAT ARE HABITS?

You could say that habits are repeated actions that we consciously or unconsciously learn. Some of the unconscious ones that we all have are things like tying our shoelaces or brushing our teeth — these are actions that we carry out without having to think about them at all. Then, there are the more conscious habits that we have built up over time, and these can be good, bad, or neutral.

I have a habit of working out every day and, although it feels very natural to me, it is actually something that I set my mind on achieving many years ago. If I skip a day for any reason and don't work out, I am very conscious of that and feel that something is missing. If you run or go to the gym every day, then you will know exactly what I am talking about.

I also have the bad habit of overworking myself, which is something I plan to change because I know that it's a relentless cycle to get into. Then, I suppose, I have many neutral habits, like parking in the same spot in my garage every day or wearing a pair of shoes. That's just me, and if I did any of the latter differently, it wouldn't seriously affect me in any way.

We are people of habit, and many of them keep us safe, make us feel secure, and help us to function throughout the day. There is a reason that we develop habits, and we now know how the brain creates them, filters them, and stores them. Your brain is the perfect machine and is very efficient when it comes to helping you achieve your goals. It basically stores your repeated actions in an area called the basal ganglia — think of this as the back office of a company, busily carrying out administrative tasks that you don't want to have to think about all the time.

The neural pathways in this region of the brain work with the frontal lobe, which makes all of the executive decisions, and carry out any tasks that don't need much thought. That explains why we don't need to pay conscious attention to many of the activities that we carry out on any given day. To do so would be impossible anyway, so our brain has mastered the art of handling most things on automatic pilot, allowing us to be involved in other activities that need our focused attention.

The more you carry out these activities, the stronger the pattern, which explains why we say that habits are hard to break. In effect, they are, because the more you do them, the deeper they become entrenched in your neural network. But that doesn't mean we can't change them and this isn't an excuse for continuing bad habits. All it takes is for us to look at the whole cycle of habit-forming behavior that we have gotten used to and learn how to intercept that. Once we do so, we can work at making it more beneficial to our well-being.

Types of habits

In essence, habits can be categorized into those which are passive, and those which are active. The passive ones arise when we are exposed often enough to situations until we eventually get used to them. Freedivers can stay under-water without any problem for much longer than you or me because their body has gradually adapted to being able to function under such conditions. Their heart rate and metabolic processes slow down, with blood going to the vital organs, helping them to dive without any equipment for sustained periods. It's an amazing feat of nature, enjoyed by whales and dolphins too!

The shoe-tying example is a good case of an active habit. At first, we have to really try hard to learn how to tie laces, and we can only do so by repeating the process many times until we get it. Once we've mastered the skill, we don't need to think about it anymore. You can tie your shoelaces blindfolded after such repetition, and even do more sophisticated things like ride a bike or play the guitar without having to concentrate at all. Habits can lead us to be more creative too, allowing us to push the boundaries of what we thought was possible and open up new avenues for us to explore, so they can be very useful.

Usually, habits are formed when they are repeated often enough, but also when there is a reward at the end. You eat healthily because you care about your body and work out because you want to stay fit — those are the rewards for your behavior. The more effort you put into these habits, the greater the reward. By the same token, bad habits bring negative outcomes. The longer you smoke, the more likely you are to suffer from some kind of lung disease later on in life. That's not a reward — it's a direct result of your bad habit and is harmful to you, even though you find it difficult to quit.

In terms of good habits, every time we practice them, we get a nice hit of dopamine, released by neurons in the limbic system that also work closely with the back office — the basal ganglia. Just imagine: the better habits you adopt, the better you will feel, which is a great incentive in itself to begin looking at ways of kicking those bad habits and adopting newer, more positive ones. Habits can be the "make or break" in your life and can lead to success or failure, so it's important to learn how you can use them to your advantage.

How to make or break a habit

There is plenty of research about how animals can be trained to behave a certain way when they learn that, by carrying out one action, they will get a reward at the end. The behavioral scientist B.F. Skinner was a pioneer in such research and his work, as well as that of others, helped us to understand there are three primary factors that lead us to form habits: **stimulus (or trigger), behavior, and reward.** The idea is that when behaviors are repeated often enough in order to receive a reward, after a while those behaviors become habits.

That's how we train dogs to sit, heel, or obey other commands. When a puppy learns that if it does *X* it will get *Y* (a treat), its dopamine is already spiking when it sees *Y*. We humans work pretty much in the same way, and even just the thought of getting a reward can trigger us into action. I'm a great believer in having good habits in my life and have seen just how beneficial they can be, not only in helping me to achieve my goals, but also to build my confidence and be more resilient.

Going to the gym and working out is something I can't live without and I train every day, no matter where I am. It's not just about getting fit or flexing my biceps, which isn't bad. It's more about the discipline that training gives me and the chance to push my limits each day. Sure, there are times when I don't feel in the mood to go or my schedule is tight; but I know that if I miss one session, it's easy from then on to miss the next one, and the one after that... It's a slippery slope.

But I love working out and feeling good physically has done a lot for my self-confidence over the years. I certainly feel more able to handle situations when I am full of energy and, by pushing my limits in every workout, I have also developed more mental stamina and resilience. My background in wrestling also helped me to be competitive and to take on challenges, even when my opponent often seemed much tougher or better than I was. That's where you have to play the mental game and work through your insecurities and fears, which is something we can all do.

It's not easy to break bad habits and adopt new ones, but it's not impossible either. Once you take the time to look at what you want to change, there are many ways to go about doing just that. Like everything else, it just needs a commitment from you to want to change; and once you take that first step, you won't regret it.

It has been said that it takes about 66 days to establish a new habit when you practice something for 30 minutes a day. That's great news because it is quite a short amount of time and is completely doable, so today is a good day to begin. You may be holding on to some old bad habits, and haven't really thought about how to adopt any new ones, which is why I want you to look at the list below and add to it any other goals you would like to achieve:

- Being more fit?
- Losing weight?
- Working less?
- Being a better partner?
- Building up a successful business?
- Helping others more?
- Believing in yourself?
- Anything else?

Once you have set your goals, I want you to understand the basic principles at play when it comes to making and breaking habits. The aim is to change your behavior and it doesn't have to be something dramatic. It can be very small things that lead to big results. The same applies for anything related to your self-development. If you want to bring positivity into your life or have more resilience, changing your thought patterns and mindset can be done by changing your thinking habits.

As an easy example, let's say that you want to lose a few pounds and in order to do so, you need to adjust your diet and exercise. I know that may sound like a mountain, but you can begin with really small steps until your mind gets into the loop.

First, decide on the kind of exercise you want to do. It should be something you will enjoy, whether that be swimming, walking, or going to the gym.

Next, take one small action related to your chosen exercise. If you want to run 5 miles, begin by running 1, and work up from there.

After your first mile, give yourself a pat on the back, hydrate, recover, then mentally prepare yourself for the next challenge ahead. Remember the 40% rule — you're only at 40 percent of what you are truly capable of achieving, so don't let your mind tell you otherwise.

Gradually, once you set a specific time and day for your running, you will not only get acclimated, but you will be able to run for longer, get fitter, and be one step closer to your ultimate goal.

What is really going on here?

You have created a new loop in your brain. As I said earlier, habits are formed by three primary factors: **triggers, behaviors, and rewards**.

Triggers can be anything that your brain recognizes associated with specific behavior. If you go for a run whenever you put on your running shoes, then every time you put on your running shoes, your brain knows what you are going to do next.

Behaviors are the response to the triggers. You go for a run when you put on your running shoes because that's what your brain knows you always do. It's an automatic response.

Rewards can be emotional or material — it doesn't matter which. The great sense of accomplishment you get after completing your run reinforces the habit and strengthens the connection between the trigger and the behavior.

The same process goes on when you are dealing with other aspects of your life. If you are stuck in a negative loop of self-criticism and low self-esteem, that can be habit-forming. If you criticize your appearance every time you look in the mirror, that will affect how you feel about yourself and cause you to neglect your appearance even more. It is very easy to fall into a downward spiral, but not irreversible. Instead of down-talking yourself, try saying how good you look the next time you pass a mirror, which will cause you to feel better and take more care of how you dress today.

You can direct your behavior by breaking the cycle of trigger-behavior-reward and create new habits that are in your better interest. You may have old habits that seem impossible to change; and I'm not saying it's going to be easy, because the more ingrained they are, the more effort will be needed to alter them. But it can be done.

When something bad happens to you, instead of seeing that as a trigger to think negatively about yourself, intercept it and put it into context. It's not about you personally — it just happened. External events shouldn't push your self-esteem even lower. So if you meet someone who treats you badly, instead of internalizing that in a way that does you more harm, see it as their problem and not yours. As a result, you won't fall into this habit of thinking you somehow deserved it or are responsible and you will eventually become more resilient.

Stopping the cycle

Our habits are default systems: actions carried out on command as a result of association and reaction. The less we think about our habits, the more they thrive. That being the case, if we turn our attention to some of the habits we would like to change, it's easy to see how, by short-circuiting the whole process, we can intervene and reset the pattern.

I used to take my cell phone to bed with me every night. It was a bad habit that I had adopted, without thinking anything of it. I would go to bed, pick up my cell phone, scroll through my social media platforms for about half an hour and then try to go to sleep. As a result, my mind was super active, and it took me so long to get to sleep that I was finding it difficult to wake up in the morning. That had a really bad knock-on effect on my day, as you can imagine.

How did I quit that habit? I started by turning my cell phone off about an hour before I went to bed and put it in a kitchen drawer, far away from my bedroom. After that, it wasn't long before I was sleeping better and getting up at my regular time. You see, the phone was my trigger and by making it inaccessible, my behavior changed. Imagine the advantages of applying the same kind of tactic to a negative thought process that you go through!

Trigger-happy

When it comes to triggers, they are the instigators of our habitual behavior and can include anything, from where we are to who we are with. In neuroscience, each time a trigger leads to a certain response, the brain is making those connections more permanent. By removing the trigger, you remove the habit, meaning that through direct action, you can help yourself to establish new patterns of behavior — new habits.

- **Triggers can be found in sequences of events.** For example, each day you get up, have a coffee, scroll through your emails, and then hop in the shower before leaving for work. If you change the sequence, you can also change the habit. Try this instead: get up, take a shower, make breakfast, leave for work. I've changed the sequence, although the initial one — get out of bed — is the same. Once your brain gets used to this new pattern of trigger and association, you won't waste time anymore checking emails (which you can do later) and you also enjoy a wholesome breakfast.
- **Time is a powerful trigger and begins when we wake up in the morning to the sound of our alarm clock.** We normally associate certain times of the day with particular activities and can use

time to our advantage or disadvantage. If you normally leave work way past office hours, try setting a gentle reminder on your smartphone when it is the correct time to leave and snooze it until you actually DO get up and leave. Spending more time at work than you should has a detrimental effect on your personal and emotional health, so cut out that bad habit now!

- **Where you find yourself at any given moment also reinforces habits.** If you are trying to quit drinking alcohol, going to your local bar isn't going to help. Arrange to meet with friends somewhere else or plan to see a movie together, rather than putting yourself in a place where breaking your bad habit will be almost impossible to do.

- **The people that you hang out with can also trigger certain habits,** especially emotional ones, so it is important to make choices based on that fact. How about keeping the company of people who bring out the best in you, rather than the worst? Being with friends or family members who make you feel negatively about yourself can perpetuate the habit you have of thinking you are worthless. Instead, choose to be with people who support, encourage, and inspire you, or have similar interests and aspirations.

- **Your emotions can trigger many bad habits,** such as binge-eating, excessive intake of alcohol, or being mean to others, to name but a few. It's very important to be mindful of your emotions and to see where they are coming from, rather than letting them run wild, because they can be potent forces for self-harm. When you feel down, spend some time thinking about why that is so — what happened, what was said, and so on. Eventually, you will be able to pinpoint where that feeling is coming from and suppress it rationally before it leads you to reach for the bottle or kick off on your partner or best friend. You can counteract negative emotions by turning to activities that bring you joy and gratification, such as going for a walk, listening to music, or even just writing down what is on your mind. All of these are good ways to avoid self-sabotaging behavior.

True grit

Concerning mental toughness, establishing good habits is paramount and, without them, you will not be able to achieve that goal. Those habits can be achieved through hard work and you have to be prepared to put the time in. The main point is to have a goal, and although motivation is important, it can gradually wear thin. This is why you need to set up a framework of good habits that will help you to get to the end. No matter how enthusiastic you are in the beginning about achieving anything, if you lack the discipline to enforce a particular habitual behavior, you are less likely to succeed. Habits create grit — that incredible ability to keep going, no matter what the odds are, and to persevere until the end.

You could say that good habits give structure: a framework that enables you to have greater mental fortitude and more chance of success. One interesting study proved just that in a world where discipline is key, and I'm referring to the United States Military. A few years ago, Angela Duckworth, a researcher at the University of Pennsylvania, carried out a study aimed at determining what qualities help people to achieve their goals and the role of mental toughness, perseverance, and passion.

Her team studied 2,441 cadets across two classes at the West Point Military Academy, who had to complete a series of tests in the program ominously known as the "Beast Barracks." The aim of the program was to test the cadets' physical, emotional and mental capacities to the limit and Duckworth recorded scores for each cadet based on their high school rank, SAT scores, Leadership Potential Score, Physical Aptitude Exam, and Grit Scale (which measures perseverance and passion for long-term goals).

The results were not what you might expect; those cadets who scored highly on the grit scale were more likely to finish the course than those with higher academic grades or leadership potential. It appeared that when it came down to it, mental toughness was much more important in getting through the Beast Barracks than intelligence, talent, or genetics.

No matter how smart or physically strong someone is, if they don't have that grit factor, they may not succeed. It's qualities like stamina, perseverance, hard work, and being prepared to follow through that ultimately offer success and you can't make use of those without establishing good habits. By building on daily habits that help you to stick to your schedule, deal with obstacles, and avoid distractions, you are setting yourself up for success. Habits are the foundation of success because, with them, you can build efficient systems that allow you to get on with the more important tasks.

FORMING GOOD HABITS

The first thing to remember is that forming any good habit is not an overnight process — it takes time and you have to stay the course if you want to get results. As Duckworth mentioned in her TED Talk, achieving success is like running a long-distance marathon rather than a 100-meter sprint. Stamina, perseverance, and the desire to win are all you need, and having good habits will get you there.

There are many ways to embrace good habits in your life and by following some of my suggestions below, you will soon discover that by taking simple steps every day, you can develop a lifestyle that allows you to pursue your dreams with greater balance and fortitude. I want you to remember that it is the smaller changes that bring about the greatest results in the long run and having a schedule can really provide the ground support that you need. It doesn't matter if you fail in the beginning — just give yourself a nudge and keep going, one step at a time.

Know your triggers

Many things can make you feel stressed, and when you go into that mode, you are unable to deal with situations rationally and calmly. That's why it's a great idea to think about what sets off your stress alarms, and either avoid them or prepare better in advance. Equally important, think about your feel-good triggers and engage in any activity that brings you fulfillment whenever you can.

Improve your physical health

I don't need to tell you how important it is to eat healthily and look after your physical health. When you eat the right food for your body and are physically fit, you have more energy to confront challenges. Avoid buying over-processed foods next time you shop and go for fresh, seasonal produce or high-energy foods instead.

View problems as temporary

Whenever a problem arises, learning to see it as a temporary setback will help you to maintain momentum. Resilient people simply deal with hurdles and move on, without losing their motivation and drive.

Don't take it personally

Stop the habit of taking everything to heart when things go wrong. Instead, embrace it and own up to whatever you feel responsible for but don't torture yourself — resilient people don't do that.

Develop an optimistic outlook

Believing that things will work out in the end will give you the impetus to keep going, and this is a habit that you can also apply to all aspects of your life. Instead of dwelling on what can go wrong, begin to think of everything that will go right, and believe in your abilities to make that happen.

Make a daily schedule

When you get up in the morning, make a small list of things you need to do today and allow time in between for meals and rest. This will help you to focus on your goals and remove the stress brought on by bad time management.

Be organized

Get into the habit of having a place for everything, so that you know where to find things when you need them. Just as chefs like to cook with a clear workbench, remove clutter or items that may distract you, which will help you to focus on what is important.

Get out more

Make a habit of getting some fresh air at least once a day. No matter what your situation, being outdoors will help you to clear your head and switch off from responsibilities and pressures, allowing you to find calmness and balance.

Sleep well

Sleep is extremely important because it regulates our cognitive and emotional functions, so establish the habit of going to bed at a set time. Remove anything from the room that can disturb you and make sure to keep it as dark as possible. Avoid stimulants before bed such as caffeine or alcohol and set the thermostat to a comfortable temperature if possible. Regular sleep patterns will give you the energy you need to approach any challenge with greater clarity.

Commit to the cause

Whatever it is that you wish to achieve, committing is a good habit to help you keep on track. You can write down your reasons for chasing a goal or create a mission statement and stay focused on that, without getting distracted by incidental events or the opinions of others.

Control what you can

You can't control everything in life, so stop thinking that you can. Concentrate on dealing with things that are in your control and you will be much more effective than if you try to manipulate situations that are out of your hands. This is just frustrating and time-wasting.

Embrace diversity

When faced with diverse viewpoints or situations, develop an attitude of openness rather than shutting down. Resilience comes from being able to handle uncertainties and leaving your comfort zone now and again. There is nothing to fear and you may even learn something useful from that experience.

Learn from mistakes

Mistakes are not failures — they are just speed bumps and learning to deal with them is important if you want to build mental resilience. Whenever you meet a bump in that road, stop to think about what went wrong, learn your lesson, and proceed with renewed wisdom.

Take time out

We all need time to step away from our responsibilities for a while and this is one habit that you should definitely nurture. Set your alarm for a specific time in the day when you can switch off for five, ten, or fifteen minutes and simply relax. Recharge your mental or emotional battery and store up energy for the rest of the day.

Ask for feedback

This is a useful tool for getting a better idea of what you can improve on or where changes can be made. You don't have to take everyone's advice, but it will help you to gain perspective on how you might do things differently and it's well worth a shot. Asking for help is also a good habit to develop and resilient people do this a lot. It's not a sign of being weak or incompetent and don't forget that iron sharpens iron!

Let go of the past

Many of us have the bad habit of going over past events and using them as benchmarks for future successes or failures. This cycle needs to end because the past is exactly that and has no bearing on your future goals and chances of achieving them. Whenever old memories of failure or negative experiences come into your mind, simply shut them down by focusing on your achievements and future goals. Make a declaration to yourself that you will not be held down by your past and will conquer what you set out to accomplish.

Be patient

Patience is not only a virtue, but a truly empowering habit to nurture. Having patience will help you to move forward without getting frustrated about things not happening sooner. Staying the course requires the ability to pace yourself and not expect to cross the finish line before the starting whistle has been blown.

Practice self-compassion

Sometimes, we can be very hard on ourselves and over-critical, placing higher expectations on our own heads than we would on others. Get into the habit of forgiving yourself for mistakes or weaknesses and focus on your positive qualities. By nurturing and learning to love your inner self, you will be better equipped to act with confidence and compassion towards others.

I hope that you will find all of the strategies listed above useful when thinking about aspects of your life that can benefit from changing habits. Being mentally resilient means having a solid framework to rely on because, if you live in chaos, your output will also be chaotic. Having good habits isn't just about order though; it's also one of the basic foundations of everyday life that allows you to confront challenges, overcome obstacles, and achieve the result that you want.

As a reminder of why good habits are so important, remember that almost 50% of the actions you carry out each day are habits. They are neurologically stored and can be changed by breaking the cycle of trigger, behavior, and reward. Your brain doesn't care if your habits are good or bad, so you can take control of them if they aren't serving you. Building new habits takes time, but it's totally doable, and good habits are your third piece of armor to add to the ones you have already started to acquire!

In the next few pages, we are going to look at what it means to be vulnerable and how embracing vulnerability can help you to overcome many issues in life that may be holding you back. I think it's fitting to end this chapter with a very inspiring quote by Brené Brown, who stated,

---

"Vulnerability is not winning or losing; it's having the courage to show up and be seen when we have no control

over the outcome. Vulnerability is not weakness; it's our greatest measure of courage."

— BRENÉ BROWN

See you in the next chapter!

4

ARMOR PIECE 4 — VULNERABILITY

Have you ever had one of those dreams where you are standing in the middle of a crowded street, completely naked? The sense of terror that comes over you when thinking that you may be fully exposed is quite scary, isn't it? After all, nobody likes to feel vulnerable, and we will do whatever it takes to avoid that feeling. I'm not suggesting that walking around naked should be encouraged, but it's a great example of the fear and shame that we experience when we feel open to criticism, attack, or rejection.

Thanks to Brené Brown, a research professor at the University of Houston and a well-known author and motivational speaker, the sensitive subject of vulnerability has really been hit out of the ballpark. In her work, Brown talks about courage, vulnerability, shame, and empathy in the same breath, opening up the dialogue on how being vulnerable is a positive trait to have, rather than something we should try to avoid. By being vulnerable, we can form deeper connections with others and experience greater joy in our lives. It takes courage to do so, but once you can, you will discover your authentic self and see life from a new perspective. In short, being vulnerable is a strength.

But what is vulnerability on a personal level, and how can we overcome it to lead happier, more fulfilled lives? As we go through this chapter, you will learn more about how being vulnerable can bring you greater emotional connections and help you overcome anything that has been holding you back up to now. We'll also take a look at the "victim" mentality you may have adopted, and work through strategies to combat such a debilitating mindset. Learning how to be vulnerable may sound frightening, which is exactly why you need to face it. Once you do, you will have acquired the fourth piece of armor that you need to strengthen your mental resilience.

The word "vulnerability" comes from the Latin word *vulnus*, or "wound." It literally means *being open to injury*, so it seems obvious that it's something undesirable. None of us want to be hurt and it's an instinctive survival technique to avoid danger and pain, right? Here, we are talking about emotional vulnerability, like when you openly express your feelings for someone without knowing what their response will be. Putting yourself out there can be so intimidating that many people do the opposite and close up completely. They prefer not to take the risk of being rejected or hurt and find it difficult to express what they feel or think because of this fear.

Traditionally, we've been brought up to hide our feelings — especially as men. We have this idea that being vulnerable is a sign of weakness or gullibility in some way. I bet that no one ever told you that it's OK to open up and share whatever it is you are going through. Being vulnerable is therefore not likely to be a behavior that you feel comfortable with. The thought of it can cause increased anxiety and shame, with so many unknowns that you would rather just not go there. I can understand why you feel like that, and I, myself, learned to bottle up many of my emotions because letting them out in the open felt like the worst thing that could possibly happen.

MY OWN PERSONAL STORY

After suffering from sexual abuse, I was afraid to seek any kind of help or even mention it and kept everything buried inside me instead. By the time I got to 6th grade, my mom was diagnosed with schizophrenia so I couldn't turn to her, and my dad was gone working most of the time. Sadly, we had developed a disconnect at this point in our relationship and I didn't feel that I could turn to him with what I was facing. I felt embarrassed, which is why I was terrified to say anything; what would people think of me if they knew what happened to me? I was battling with my own mind, and this left me feeling totally alone. Going into my sophomore year of high school, my parents divorced and, shortly after, my mom moved away. Everything just pushed me to the edge, and it got to the point where I even contemplated taking my own life. I was tired of being bullied by older kids on the dead-end street where I was living, and a recent heartbreak had left me feeling totally alone. It seemed as if no one loved me or cared about me and I didn't see any point in living. I was done.

I had a very hard time concentrating in school and had developed a bad stutter after the abuse happened when I was younger. This lack of concentration and stuttering continued through high school and had an extremely negative impact on how I felt about myself. Wrestling did help in many ways, but the pain was so deep, even that couldn't save me. Feeling alone and unworthy, I decided one night that I'd had enough and around 2 a.m., committing suicide was the only thing on my mind.

Then something weird happened. I felt this urge to go for a run instead, so off I went, blasting Skillet in my headphones. After running for 7 miles, I stopped and dropped to my knees. At that moment, I decided to give my life to God; and so, following that night, I began attending a youth group where I became a worship drummer, which helped immensely. But even then, I still felt as if I was carrying the weight of the world on my shoulders and wanted to be free. I didn't know how to achieve this, so I decided to go on an 11-month, 11-country Christian mission trip known as The World Race.

It seemed like the right thing for me to do at the time, and I am grateful that I did, because in 2012, I had a breakthrough. I finally managed to share my abuse story with my squad while on The World Race, and a friend on the mission trip recommended I read a book called *Redeeming Love* by Francine Rivers. After taking her advice, I started to genuinely experience God's love for me and began to see myself as worthy, rather than unworthy. I managed to find the courage, after about a year, to tell my wife, who I was dating at the time, and eventually told my immediate family.

The funny thing is that the more I began to tell people about what had happened to me, the more freedom I started to experience. It was a really liberating process, which also involved forgiving the person who committed these terrible acts. I can say in all honesty that it took me a very long time to get to a place in my life where I felt secure about myself. I hadn't even realized how many other people have endured sexual abuse as a child until I started speaking out about it. By doing so, it allowed me to open the door for others to find the courage to talk about their abuse and overcome those terrible feelings of being alone and ashamed. It has given me great joy to be able to help others experience the same freedom and hope for the future as I have, because no one should ever have to go through that pain.

The support of my wife and family throughout this journey has been a cornerstone, and I cannot thank them enough for that. Choosing to live a positive and proactive life, as well as being involved in an active church community, has helped me grow and overcome the negativity and dark path I could have been led down. The odds were surely against me, but through faith and choosing to live a life of happiness, I released myself from that bondage and conquered my fears.

WHAT IS VULNERABILITY?

As humans, we are, by nature, inherently vulnerable, and that's just the way things are. Apart from the fear of physical harm, which can be life-saving, our core psychological vulnerability is very ingrained in us. For many reasons, we have learned to be fearful of making the wrong decisions, choosing the unknown path, and being a failure. A lot of this goes back to what I have already touched on in this book, about the need to belong and fear of rejection. In a world full of unknowns, dangers, and risks, it seems natural to want to protect ourselves from anything that can affect our existence.

But this does take its toll on our emotional well-being and can greatly affect our relationships and sense of personal worth and esteem. Instead of shielding ourselves from possible pain by leading sheltered, closed-off lives, maybe being vulnerable isn't such a bad thing after all. Sure, it can expose you to the risk of emotional harm, but it can also lead to greater mental resilience, creativity, and even redemption.

The truth is that we are all vulnerable in some ways. Everyone is exposed to daily life and what that entails: from personal relationships and health issues to unforeseen events and natural disasters. We simply can't control everything around us and, from the moment we wake up in the morning, we have no idea what the day may bring.

Emotional vulnerability is much more complicated and just the thought of being rejected by our peers can lead us to experience high levels of stress. If you are dependent on others in a care-giving situation, you are also much more likely to feel vulnerable; and if you find it difficult to express yourself, this can also add to the problem. Negative childhood experiences and traumas can eat away at your self-confidence over time and diminish your ability to trust others, causing you to avoid any situation in which you may feel vulnerable. This can have a severely damaging effect on your quality of life and the relationships that you form.

As you can see from the above, the impact of fearing vulnerability can play a massive part in how you live your life. You may purposefully avoid certain people or situations and not pursue your goals or dreams because of it. In a nutshell, you are not living to your full potential.

Why you should be vulnerable

I want you to believe me when I say that being vulnerable is NOT a bad thing. On the contrary: It is an extremely useful trait that you just need to approach the right way, and that's the paradox.

As Brené Brown so rightly pointed out, vulnerability is the first thing we look for in others and the last thing we want to see in ourselves. You may immediately spot it in friends and family but pretend that it doesn't apply to you, and you do this by hiding it away inside. That's a crazy thing to do, and it's a pattern of behavior that is delusional, because if you really wish to get in touch with your authentic self, then you have to learn to be vulnerable. It may bring heartache, pain, and disappointment, but it can also create unimaginable joy and satisfaction in all aspects of your life. In that respect, being vulnerable isn't a weakness, but a strength.

Admitting that you aren't perfect is the first step to being vulnerable and a great place to start. When you acknowledge that you are not superman/woman, you open the door to greater self-knowledge. Recognizing your flaws and imperfections will help you to think about which areas require improvement and give you a target to work towards. Saying, "I don't know," is a springboard from which to learn something new and helps you to define your limits and expectations. If you are unwilling to explore these, how can you ever progress? It's OK to tell yourself that you don't know everything because no one else does either!

Everyone has weaknesses and often, by opening up about your fears and doubts to someone else, you can establish deeper, more meaningful relationships. Having superficial connections is not offering you anything and neither are you giving anything substantial back in return. The fear of rejection may be a deciding factor in your inability to bond with others, and this is something that you need to have a discussion with yourself about first. Do you want to live in fear, or face your vulnerability and move beyond it?

WHAT CAN VULNERABILITY OFFER YOU?

If the fear of opening up terrifies you, then you need to confront that. Closing up may seem like a safer option but in the long run, you are doing yourself more harm than good. Keeping your struggles to yourself and putting on a brave face may seem like the logical thing to do, but it's the easy way out. There's nothing tough about ignoring your problems, which is essentially what you are doing by refusing to open up to others. I know just as much as anyone how hard it is to sit down and talk about how you are feeling or what you are going through. But if you don't do that, you will continue to suffer alone. Victims of abuse often take this stance, burying past events so deeply within themselves that they can even reach a state of denial about the abuse ever taking place. It's very painful to bring up those memories and share them with someone else, even with a trained professional, as there is so much guilt and shame involved.

What you need to know is that most people struggle with vulnerability in some shape or form, and there is no standard rule about how serious or trivial your own personal experience is. You may want to hide from your boss the fact that you failed to complete an important report as you don't wish to hear their critical feedback, which makes you feel like even more of a failure. It could be that you have gone through extreme physical, psychological, or sexual abuse and cannot share it with anyone because of a deep sense of shame. In both cases, it has more to do with your level of self-esteem than with the other person's reaction, and the fear of being vulnerable is reinforcing that negative image of yourself.

Being open, whatever has happened, is the key to self-development, and allowing yourself to be vulnerable can bring about life-changing results.

Being open to change

If you are happy with yourself, fine. I'm not going to try to convince you to change if you believe you have everything worked out. If you want to change but are afraid to, that's completely normal. We all prefer to sit in our comfort zone, even when it's not in our best interests because it just seems easier. Change requires hard work, sweat, and often tears, but I can guarantee you that it is 100% worth it. It begins when you are able to look beyond your fear and ask yourself, "What am I really afraid of?"

This could mean digging deep into your darkest emotions — that black hole you have been throwing everything bad into — but it has to be done. Think of it as similar to servicing your car — you know it's going to be costly and involve a lot of work, but the end result will be well worth the time, expense, and effort. You get better performance, more security, and the knowledge that you have just added a few more years to your car's lifespan. You get peace of mind!

Gaining new perspectives

We tend to think that our experiences are more serious or significant than what others have gone through and often stick to that belief as though it's a life raft in the middle of the ocean. But guess what… sharing those experiences with others may just give you more perspective as you compare your problems with theirs and perhaps find common ground. You will discover that you are not alone in your problems and may also gain insight into ways of dealing with them. There is nothing scary about that, right?

I know that you have probably built up a very distinct construct in your mind about who you are and what you are capable of; and often events that have occurred can become highly magnified within such a construct, accruing greater significance than they deserve. If you are willing to be vulnerable, just for five minutes, you may hear different viewpoints, which could eventually broaden your horizons. The walls of your mental construct may even come tumbling down, allowing you to rebuild a healthier, more positive self.

The process of healing

To heal, you have to be prepared to acknowledge that there is a problem. No one can help you to resolve any issues that you have unless you can open up and talk about them. Fear of being judged, criticized, or shamed may prevent you from revealing your wounds to others and those fears stem from something way back in your past that you have never confronted. It takes guts to sit down and talk about your story; but the truth is that everyone has a story, and you are never alone in that respect.

When wounds are covered up for too long, they can fester and rot. They need fresh air to aid the healing process, and this is exactly the same with emotional pain. Suppressing it eventually leads to a build-up of bitterness that poisons your relationships and causes even greater internal stress. By learning to express what is going on in a safe environment, you can begin to heal and walk through life with unwavering confidence.

Being authentic

If you have an intense fear of being vulnerable, you may distance yourself from others and find it hard to maintain meaningful relationships. You will never be able to establish close bonds if you aren't prepared to reveal your authentic self because that is what all healthy relationships are based on. Allow others to get to know you by uncovering parts of yourself that you judge to be unsightly and let them learn to love the real you.

You need to develop trust if you wish to achieve this, and it begins by trusting in yourself. You are not the person responsible for any negative experiences in your life and need to realize that those external events don't define you. If it is the case that you have done something terrible in your past, such as committing a serious crime that you have served time for, that is OK too. Self-forgiveness is an important step on the way to forming new connections and you will discover that others are more than willing to accept you for who you are.

Overcoming vulnerability

There are many obstacles in our way when trying to overcome vulnerability, some of which are created by our own self-illusion, and all are based on fear. One of the strongest obstacles is the fear of not belonging, which causes us to hide and not reveal our true selves. Shame is also a strong deterrent that prevents us from opening up and revealing our pain. Whether the stigma is real or not, the sense of shame can be a terrible burden to carry, and the longer you do so, the heavier it becomes. Previous traumas can stop us from sharing anything about our life story with others because we fear that we will be judged or criticized. It can also simply be very painful to bring up such memories if we have not learned how to come to terms with them. A lack of confidence and self-esteem can also prohibit us from facing our fear of vulnerability, and this requires a lot of self-work beforehand.

It may seem like an impossible task to come to grips with, but facing your fear of vulnerability has already begun as you read this chapter. Here are my top ten strategies to use as you take on the challenge:

1. Building walls blocks progress. The higher the wall, the more isolated you will feel, and others will be less able to reach you.
2. Your fear of vulnerability may be causing pain to others, who want to be close to you and are being pushed away.
3. Being distant is not the way to nurture closer, deeper relationships.
4. Learning to love yourself and accepting who you are is the best way to overcome your fear of vulnerability.
5. Self-criticism is your worst enemy and only you are so hard on yourself. Most people don't dwell on your flaws or remember the last time you made a "mistake."
6. Holding yourself up rather than dragging yourself down will help you to be more resilient, no matter what cards life has dealt you.
7. Everyone makes mistakes and by acknowledging them, you are embracing your humanity. Torture yourself over what you did or didn't do in the past if you like, but learning how to respond in the future is more productive.
8. You don't need to prove anything to anyone other than yourself. If you nurture a greater sense of self-esteem, you can be your own mentor.
9. Be prepared to open up to others and if you are met with disrespect, remove yourself from that situation. Stick with people who give you loving support instead.

10. Free yourself from the need to bury your past.
    Instead, accept it and move on. Your history is
    important and can make you stronger, wiser, and
    happier.

Instead of being fearful of your vulnerability, you could try embracing it. That sounds risky, I know. But what is life without taking a few risks? When water sits stagnant in a pond for a long time, it becomes a breeding ground for all kinds of nasty bacteria, making it totally unsuitable for drinking. On the other hand, a free-flowing river is full of life and vibrant energy, gathering momentum as it gushes along to meet the vast, infinite ocean. Which one would you prefer to be: the pond or the river?

I have another question for you. How often have you said to yourself, "It's not my fault"? I imagine that if you have gone through tough times, you are perfectly justifiable in saying this, especially if you were a victim of some kind of abuse or wrongdoing. But often, people will make the "it's not my fault" statement to avoid taking any responsibility for their lives.

This is known as a **victim mentality,** which is based on the pretext that bad things happen and will keep on happening. People with this mindset always blame others or a set of circumstances for whatever is going on and don't try to create change because they believe they will be unsuccessful. Having this type of thought pattern is not the same as fear of vulnerability, which is built on shutting down from any action or dialogue that has the potential to expose us. The victim is more than happy to talk about what happened to them and always puts the blame on someone or something else for their predicament.

WHAT IS THE VICTIM MENTALITY?

As a victim, you may feel vulnerable and, because you get into this mindset of feeling weak or helpless, you begin to believe that you are. This can lead you to comply with anyone who appears stronger or more persuasive than yourself, hence reinforcing the feeling of being unable to figure things out on your own. It's kind of a vicious cycle that keeps you locked in the mindset of not being able to take control of your life.

It's easier to play the victim than take responsibility into your own hands, which requires a lot of effort and facing up to some truths. But I know that if you have a victim mindset, it's not something that you do intentionally. It's a behavior that you have learned to protect yourself from dealing with painful past experiences. I'm not here to judge you, but to give you a helping hand with coping mechanisms that you can use to see life from a more positive perspective. Once you begin to do that, you will gain more control and stop depending on others to set the limits on what you can or can't do.

Nobody ever chooses to be a victim and most people who have a victim mentality have developed it as a way of dealing with some kind of trauma that they have undergone. If you have experienced any emotional pain, this may have created a feeling of helplessness and of being trapped. If you have ever been betrayed or let down, that can also make you feel like a victim, and you will find it very hard to trust anyone. Maybe you have adopted the habit of sacrificing your own well-being to support your partner, parent, or friend, which leaves you feeling frustrated and resentful. Constantly blaming others for any problems, you might even use manipulation to get sympathy or attention.

Having this kind of mindset makes life very difficult, and bad things will continue to happen because you have chosen to give up. If you don't aspire to achieve anything, based on the belief that nothing goes your way, then it is very likely that you will never successfully reach any goals. So, we have to change that way of thinking, as it isn't helping you at all.

Bad things happen to everyone, and we need to see what, if any, responsibility we have for such events. If your car keeps getting stolen because you never bother to lock it, then you have some responsibility to share in that, right? It doesn't mean that you are to blame for the thieves' actions; it just means stepping up to prevent it from happening in the first place or at least make it more difficult.

Usually, if you have a victim mentality, you will find it difficult to seek out solutions to problems and will even refuse help when it's offered. If you blame other people or circumstances for anything that happens to you, you won't feel able to correct the situation or improve on it. You probably feel powerless to change anything and will even practice negative self-talk and self-sabotage. This in itself means that things can easily spiral out of control, as you make reaffirming statements like:

> *Bad things always happen to me.*
> *I can't do anything about it.*
> *There's no point in trying.*
> *No one cares about me.*

Getting out of that cycle is imperative if you want to move on to a more fulfilling life and it all begins with developing greater self-confidence and self-esteem, which we have already covered in this book. Mental resilience comes when we practice flexing those muscles and cut out any negative self-talk that is holding us back. You have the power to achieve this and adopting habits to help you on your way is very important. One thing is certain: if you try to improve your situation, things will get easier in time. Even failure will be seen as a small trip-up and eventually, you will see life through a new lens, full of positivity and possibilities.

Carrying on with a victim mindset can be harmful to you and those around you, so it's vital to take the time to see how your thoughts are affecting your life. On an emotional level, I am sure that you will often feel frustrated, angry, hopeless, resentful, and hurt. Such feelings can lead to angry outbursts, depression, loneliness, and isolation. It's not easy to overcome that behavior, but getting to the root cause can help you enormously. Working through chronic long-term victim mentality can be very tricky to do on your own and if you don't have a good support network of family or friends willing to help, it's not easy to confront your demons. You may need the help of a trained professional to do this, and there is absolutely no shame in that.

Much of what you experience may be learned helplessness that goes back to your childhood or early adulthood, being raised in an environment that encouraged dependence rather than independence. You might have been bullied at school or mistreated by a figure of authority, for example. It's a painful process to work out exactly where your victimhood is coming from, but once you unravel that, you are on the way to addressing the issues and moving on.

What you can do today is begin to implement the strategies below to help you overcome this negative mindset and start to take charge of your life:

Challenge any limiting beliefs

Your beliefs about yourself are perceptions created by past memories that you have formed over time and emotionalized. If you can identify them, you can see which ones are making you feel like a victim. When did you first begin to feel self-pity in your life? What happened in your younger years that triggered this reaction? Spend some time thinking about this and once you put your finger on when those feelings started, you can change the narrative.

Take ownership of your life

Taking ownership means being responsible for your thoughts, feelings, and actions. Life is in your hands, not in the hands of someone else and you can create the one that YOU want. Instead of blaming someone else, assume responsibility and be a winner, not a victim. You owe it to yourself!

Be grateful

Instead of complaining about what is missing in your life, be thankful for what you have. When you consciously express gratitude for things that bring you joy, you will begin to appreciate how fortunate you are. Give thanks for one small thing every night before you go to sleep and when you wake up in the morning, notice how much better it instantly makes you feel.

Be positive

Don't surrender to negative thoughts, because they will only bring you down. Focus on positives to attract more good things into your life. On a cloudy day, look for the silver lining and after the rain, wait for the rainbow. Do this simple thing and your life will shift from negativity to abundance and positivity.

Learn to forgive

When you learn to forgive, you are releasing yourself from the hold that another person has on you, and that is extremely liberating. If you can find a way to forgive someone who has done you harm, you will remove the layers of pain they caused you and carry on throughout life with a sense of tranquility.

Focus on helping others

Shifting your attention from yourself and diverting your energy to helping others serves two aims: firstly, it can remind you of how blessed you are in many ways; and secondly, the more you give to others, the more you receive. As an extra bonus, by being kind to others, you will also be more compassionate with yourself.

Be a survivor

The victors are the ones who survive, not those who sit feeling sorry for themselves. Why do that when you can feel good, despite what you have been through? Be an inspiration to others and a beacon of light rather than misery. Cherish all of the good things that you have experienced and give thanks instead of complaining about the bad. Adopt a survivor's mindset and keep going because life is meant to be lived to the fullest.

Embodying a victim mindset can set you up for failure, so when you meet obstacles in your way, you are unable to move forward. If you adopt a challenge perspective instead, each hurdle is an opportunity for growth and self-development. See the problem as something that just happened, rather than saying that it happened "to you," and remove all of the emotional baggage that might pile up.

It's the challenges we face in life that give us the will to persevere, and this creates a positive cycle that boosts our resilience. Everyone loves seeing their favorite team bounce back from a run of losses to a triumphant victory, so follow that example. Authenticity is equally important although it's not easy to practice because it requires openness and honesty. It involves knowing yourself, which takes time and effort, but this is the additional piece of armor that will bring you even greater inner balance. With it, you will discover a life full of meaning and purpose even if it is mixed with suffering and joy. Embrace it all!

Being aware of yourself is one thing, but developing the skills to take in what is going on around you and make the best decisions based on that is also very important. If you are confident in your abilities and can focus on your goal, you will make it happen. There are ways to nurture that focus and we will learn more in the next chapter, as well as discover some useful strategies to guarantee you success.

I'll leave you with an interesting quote by Sean McVay, the youngest guy ever to have been made head coach of a National Football League team at the age of 30 and awarded the title of Coach of the Year during his time with the Los Angeles Rams.

Talking about what makes a great player, he commented:

"When you look at what we want our individual player to represent..., we're looking for mentally and physically tough players who are smart and want to compete. And when you say smart, you're talking about situational awareness. Guys that are instinctual. That are smart football players."

— SEAN MCVAY

That's something to think about as we head on to the next chapter.

5

ARMOR PIECE 5 — TUNNEL-VISION FOCUS

We all admire people who do high-risk jobs, like pilots, firefighters, and brain surgeons, who are expected to perform with a 0% fail rate. One slip-up can be devastating in these instances, not only for the person carrying out the task but also for those involved. You can imagine the scene if a pilot isn't paying attention to his instrument panel because he is too busy chatting to his co-pilot about plans for the weekend or if a surgeon gets distracted for a millisecond by a scalpel falling to the floor.

These kinds of jobs require a high degree of focus and concentration. You just can't afford to be elsewhere mentally when you are carrying out neuro-surgery or running into a blazing building. These men and women are our heroes: portraying bravery, expertise, and skill. So, how do they manage to deal with such intense situations? What's their superpower, and can you get it too?

Here's the thing: it's not some rare character trait that most of us mere mortals can never possess. It's a soft skill called **situational awareness** and, just like any other skill, it can be learned, built, and refined with experience.

You may be wondering what use it is to you in your everyday life. You probably don't have a high-risk job and you're not a secret agent or air-traffic controller, so why should you worry about having situational awareness? That's a good question and one I am going to answer in this chapter.

Since we are talking about the fifth piece of mental armor, which is **tunnel-vision focus**, it's important to understand how being more aware of what is going on around you can help you to focus on what is important at any given time. Having the ability to make a balanced assessment of the situation you are in will ensure that you make better decisions and stay aligned with the goals you have set for yourself. In that respect, situational awareness is a valuable life tool.

If you develop better situational awareness, you can manage information easier, interpret it more efficiently, and use it to your advantage. This is intelligent decision-making and you can benefit from it in all aspects of your life. It can be useful in a work environment, in your relationships, and regarding your future ambitions or goals.

Basically, it means that you have greater control and can acquire a better outcome every time.

One of the reasons that you may be failing in certain aspects of your life could be because you lose focus, and that's a perfectly normal occurrence for many people. With everything going on around us, filtering out what needs our attention and being able to prioritize can be a headache. We are bombarded with so many stimuli these days and an infinite number of distractions. Sometimes, it can feel impossible to carry out a simple task like writing an email, never mind completing a life goal. I get it — we are all guilty of getting sidetracked by other things that crop up during our day and it can seem impossible to focus on a task we need to do, or a target we want to reach.

That's where prioritizing comes in, because if you can learn to select what you need to focus on, then you stand a much better chance of being successful. I learned this at an early age when I got involved in wrestling, and most athletes will know what I'm talking about here. When I used to walk out onto the mat to face my opponent, I could obviously see the crowd, my team, and the coach, but when it came time to wrestle, the only thing I honed in on was the guy in front of me. My sole aim at that point was to defeat him and nothing else was on my mind. I was totally engrossed in winning the match and all of my attention was on that, nothing else.

This is the kind of "in the zone" mentality that a lot of athletes use and I'll talk about it in greater length later. For now, I want to talk more about situational awareness and how to apply it. A key concept in any domain where the human factor plays a significant role, such as in aviation, command and control, or crisis management, situational awareness is a function of the human brain and how it responds to complex, dynamic, or high-risk settings. You could say that it describes the mental model of a decision-maker in an evolving task situation and it's not difficult to see how it is an essential skill in certain occupations.

It's also a tool that you can use in everyday life. When you have a goal in mind or something that you want to accomplish, situational awareness can really up your game because it allows you to grasp an awareness and understanding of the "environment" and other factors that may affect your goals. What you need is rapid and appropriate decisions and effective actions, which you won't have if you don't observe what is going on around you.

Not having this skill can lead to mistakes, and a lack of situational awareness has been identified as one of the main reasons for accidents caused by human error. In that sense, it's a way of avoiding mishaps and achieving what you have set out to do successfully. There are hundreds of examples of situations going wrong because the participants weren't completely aware of all the conditions that could impact their decisions. Just think of the devastating number of air traffic accidents caused by pilot error, for example, and you can appreciate what I mean. These are extreme cases, but a lack of situational awareness can also have a direct impact on everyone's lives, no matter what they are involved in.

It all comes down to having the right mindset of knowing what's going on around you at that moment. Now, you are reading this book, and not thinking about the argument you had yesterday, or the chores you have to do tomorrow. Yet, you are still aware of the noises outside, the weather, who is with you, what that person is doing. You made a decision based on these factors and prioritized what you want or need to do. If it suddenly starts raining, you may have to close the windows and if your cell phone rings, you may choose to ignore it. That's a simple way to describe how you use situational awareness daily, so you are capable of it. When it comes to your life goals and dreams, you can also apply the same robust technique to help you achieve success.

Imagine that you have set off on a road trip across the States on your newly acquired Harley-Davidson but don't have that much experience. If you aren't aware of what's going on around you, there are several risks and dangers, many of which can be life-threatening or at least cut your journey short. You need to have a perception of elements in the environment, such as the weather and road conditions at any given moment. You need to be able to interpret what they mean and project their status in the near future so that you can anticipate any problems ahead. In short, you need situational awareness, which contains three levels: perception, comprehension, and projection.

1. Perception

Having perception means that you can gather information from everything that is going on around you. It's like having a bird's eye view of the terrain and a 360-degree viewpoint. During your road trip, you need to be continuously monitoring weather conditions, traffic, your bike's performance, how you are feeling physically, and any other factors to ensure a safe journey. It's this perception that will help you to achieve your goal.

2. Comprehension

Comprehension relates to the way you understand and analyze information around you. Grasping what is happening and being able to interpret that correctly will help you to make the right decision. If you see a traffic pile-up ahead while on your road trip, you know that you have to slow down. Ignoring those dark clouds that signal heavy rain or a strange noise coming from your engine can seriously affect your journey, so being able to successfully analyze cues is extremely important.

3. Projection

How good are you at predicting outcomes based on information from your surroundings? Being able to make projections about the future based on what you know now doesn't require a crystal ball. It takes a good grasp of what is happening at this moment so that you can confidently react to any hurdle or challenge ahead. Going full speed down Route 66 on your Harley is great, but being able to predict what will happen if you have to brake suddenly is definitely something that you should have mastered if you want to stay in one piece.

As you can see, perception, comprehension, and projection are not impossible skills to acquire. You simply need to perfect them so that you can set about achieving your goals with a better chance of success. Having a greater sense of situational awareness is not a guarantee of anything, because there will always be other factors that can sabotage your efforts. You may suffer from a lot of stress, have financial difficulties, or relationship problems. All of these can seem difficult to control and may occupy your mind, leaving less space for situational awareness to develop. If you are on any kind of meds, this can also affect your ability to function, so don't be too hard on yourself if you find the concept difficult to apply at first.

Give yourself a chance to ease into the idea gradually and remove any self-imposed limitations that could hold you back. It doesn't require you to make a major overhaul in your life; and just by thinking about the idea, you can slowly sharpen your skills and reach a point where it will be useful. You can begin by following the key steps below and see how you progress:

PRACTICE YOUR POWERS OF PERCEPTION

This is a good place to start and can be done easily. Begin by paying attention to your surroundings, using all of your senses. Don't just look, but listen, smell, and touch... see how many things you would have missed otherwise. The more you practice doing this, the more you will get into the habit of being aware of your environment. An example that comes to mind is when my wife and I were driving on the freeway in the far-left lane, next to the carpool lane. The flow of traffic was much slower than in the carpool lane and I noticed the driver in front of us looked left multiple times because it seemed like she wanted to attempt to get into that lane. As soon as I realized what was playing out, I slowed down to create a good amount of distance between us and this vehicle, and then the worst happened. I looked back and as I did so, I saw a vehicle speeding along the carpool lane while the driver in front of me rushed into the lane and got struck. I had to slam on my brakes and luckily, we were fine, although two other vehicles in front of us got pretty smashed up. By perceiving what was happening, I prepared myself for the worst and came out of it unscathed.

Manage stress overload

Stress causes chaos because it prohibits your brain from functioning rationally. Even in a crisis situation, professionals have to keep their heads; otherwise, lives can be lost. If you suffer from stress, remember that you need to practice self-care, which includes prioritizing what you can and cannot handle. Being overworked, not eating correctly, or having insufficient sleep can all affect your coping mechanisms. Once you remove stress, you will be in a better position to react efficiently in any given situation.

Visualize yourself in future scenarios

How would you react if you suddenly lost your job or your partner? By imagining yourself in future scenarios, you will be better prepared if such an outcome occurs. I hope that none of the above examples apply to you, but it is useful to plan for any future events that might steer you off course from your goals. This will give you a heads-up to handle pitfalls because you have already walked through a mental rundown in your mind. You can't predict what is going to happen on the freeway, as my example above showed, and none of us could have foreseen that a global pandemic like COVID-19 would change the course of our collective future forever. But you can try to imagine yourself in testing situations and think about how you will respond to them.

Stop and check

A new habit worth adopting is to press the pause button at least once a day, no matter what you are doing, for a few moments. Make a quick mental assessment of what is going on around you and ask yourself things like, "What can I hear? What can I see?" It's often said that we don't take enough notice of our surroundings and we filter out a lot of cues that could be useful to us, so stop now for a second and simply observe. You will notice a lot more than you thought existed.

One technique you can apply is taken from an occupational workspace viewpoint, and it's called the **SLAM** method. It involves four steps that can be implemented in your life when you are trying to achieve an end goal and goes something like this:

STOP and think about what you are doing before you carry out any action.

LOOK around you and assess what is working for you or against you.

SLAM METHOD

ASSESS the risks and chances of success, depending on the factors involved

MANAGE the options open to you and readjust priorities if you need to.

Be prepared

Think about possible options if things don't go as you had planned. If you want to accomplish something, write down all of the things that could go wrong, and try to pinpoint how you could remedy them. You wouldn't jump out of a plane on a skydiving adventure without a parachute, would you? And what if the chute you have doesn't open? Having a second safety chute is like having a contingency plan and one that you should make sure to have with you. This can apply to most challenges in life.

Read between the lines

Nonverbal cues can help us to understand what someone is really thinking or feeling, so paying attention to those can be invaluable. Being able to interpret your boss or partner's body language can provide you with a much better assessment of their state than just by listening to what they say, and will help you know if you need to change your plan or shift priorities. After all, people don't always say what they mean or mean what they say.

Pay attention to your gut instinct

Our gut instinct is something that many of us ignore because we are so used to depending on hard-and-fast evidence, but it can be more useful than we give it credit for. When something feels wrong, it usually is. Have you ever experienced walking into a room and sensed that something wasn't right, but couldn't exactly put your finger on it? That's your gut instinct, or heightened sense of awareness, which unfortunately we don't listen to most of the time. Start paying more attention to it and you will be amazed at how useful it is in assessing situations correctly.

Situational awareness is definitely an important skill to develop because it allows you to see the bigger picture. Usually, the more we focus on the small details, the more we miss a lot of other useful things, leaving gaps in our understanding. Tunnel vision can restrict what we see and hear and curtail our perception of events, so it's not desirable if that is the outcome. While tunnel vision is supposed to help us keep focused on our goals, being too focused has its flaws. How often have you found yourself scrolling through your social media posts and not heard what someone else in the room was saying to you? This is because when your brain focuses on a visual stimulus, it tends to ignore audible messages, and this is known as auditory exclusion.

Tunnel vision can limit other areas of your life too, as it becomes a way of doing things that excludes other options. Apart from focusing on a visual activity so intensely that you don't hear or see anything else around you, you may get irritated when disturbed. It could make you inflexible and not open to suggestions even if the opinions of others could be beneficial and it may mean that you refuse help even if that would be useful. Another downside to having tunnel vision is that you might work for hours without a break, which is counter-productive in the long run. Eventually, you lose track of time and space, with other priorities being neglected.

The most effective technique involves knowing how to utilize tunnel vision to your advantage and staying focused on your goals. It's all about finding balance and the difference between getting lost in the forest and keeping your eye on the one tree that you want to reach. When you are too focused on a task, you miss other peripherals that could be important. The idea is to be aware of what is going on around you and then zoom in on the job at hand.

Be both present and focused at the same time

Being present means having an awareness of all the things going on at this moment, while still able to concentrate on what you have in mind.

This way of functioning helps you to be aware and yet fully tuned in. Imagine that it's like someone engaged in deep meditation who is still able to sense a fly that has landed on their nose... they can feel it's there, but it doesn't stop them from meditating. That takes some discipline, but it can be done. In that respect, having control over your focus is incredibly important for building mental resilience and you can achieve it in many ways.

Set daily non-negotiable routines

One of the first things I strongly advise is to establish some kind of daily non-negotiable routine, which will help you to stay focused on your goals. Instead of saying, "I'll do it tomorrow," make a time block in your day to accomplish the task. It doesn't matter what time that is, as long as it is practical and will allow you to work towards your target. Make sure you stick to the same time every day, no exceptions.

Set tangible goals

If your goal is totally unrealistic, there's no way you're going to be able to focus on it for more than five minutes.

Distinguish between what is feasible and what is just a pipe dream — I think you know the difference! That doesn't mean you can't dream big. It just requires that you take small actions every day, which will have a cumulative effect that gets you nearer to achieving your initial goal. I can share a great example of this with you from my life. I had been wanting to make a full-length rock album for years that would feature all of my own songs. At first, it seemed like an impossible task, but passion drove me forward. I took one step at a time to get there, and it was close to a year before my producer and friend Cody and I were finally able to piece it together. Now, when I listen to my own music, I can't help but feel proud of what I have accomplished because it was no easy task. You can enjoy this same experience by pursuing the things you are passionate about, one day at a time, and push yourself to attain more in your life.

Visualize your end results

If you want to pass that next training module, visualize yourself holding the certificate. Trying to save up enough money to buy a new home? Imagine yourself sitting on your new patio with an ice-cold drink or a warm cup of coffee. By visualizing and declaring victory over your end results, you are essentially tricking your brain into thinking that you have already achieved them, so you get a serotonin spike, which propels you to keep working towards them.

Help yourself to stay focused

Remind yourself what your goals are and write them down, placing them somewhere visible. That could be on your smartphone, car dashboard, or computer screen. With all of the distractions going on in life, it's easy to get waylaid, but if you give yourself visual cues often enough, they will help you to maintain that much-needed focus.

Share your vision

You don't have to go it alone, and friends or family can be a great support to help you reach your goal. Just by sharing your aspirations, you are committing to reaching for them and you will see how keen others are to support you on your mission. Having someone to back you, encourage you, and even steer you when you may be drifting away from your objective is a real advantage. In addition, by sharing your vision, you become accountable. If you have told your friends or family that you are going to do something, then it kind of ties you to keeping your word and that can motivate you even more to be successful.

Don't multitask

Multitasking is hailed as a great skill to have, but if you want to achieve something specific, your success rate drops if you have too many balls up in the air at the same time. The trick to achieving any goal is to single-task, which means doing one thing at a time. For example, when I decided to create my rock album, I put all of my energy into that until it was done. After that, I focused on developing a new product for my business, giving it 100% of my attention. If I had tried to do both simultaneously, the chances are that I would have had less enthusiasm, time, and energy to work on either, so I may never have pulled either off successfully.

Feed the machine

Your brain is the most efficient computer in the world, but it needs more than adrenaline to keep running. You must make it a priority to feed it with the right amount of quality sleep and nutritious food, and learn to breathe more slowly. Everyone knows the health benefits of a good sleep and a balanced diet, but slowing your breathing down also stills the mind, giving it time and space to serve you better. You can try simple breathing techniques for a few minutes each day and will notice the difference immediately.

If you remember, earlier on in the chapter I talked about being "in the zone," which is when you are intensely focused on something specific and have no, or very little, perception of anything else going on around you. If you see an NBA player going for that crucial free throw, you can tell that he is completely engrossed in getting the ball in the net, seemingly unaware of the noise and activity around him at that specific moment.

This is a special kind of tunnel vision in which time and sound seem to fall away and is often reported by athletes and creatives as being almost like a spiritual experience where anything is possible. The world-class endurance triathlete and ultrarunner Christopher Bergland described it as feeling as if his body became a conduit for the earth's infinite energy, propelling him forward even though he was exhausted. This heightened state arises when you feel inspired but not overwhelmed and can apply to any aspect of your life, from your workout to your career path.

To get to that "flow" state, as it is often called, you need to be constantly repurposing your mind when doing a task to get you to your intended target. If you are becoming bored or apathetic, it means that you need to change the goalposts and challenge yourself further. Being "in the zone" isn't something that you need to practice every day, but it can give you that extra push when you need to get to a certain milestone. It is usually a short-lived experience because you can't function at that level of intensity all the time, but as any successful athlete or creative person will tell you, it can be a truly rewarding experience.

The main thing I want you to take from this chapter is that having tunnel-vision focus can be a great asset, as long as it is accompanied by the skill of situational awareness. The next time you embark on a project, consider all of the parameters present: the time needed to accomplish it, the tools you will need, the knowledge required, as well as any possible outcomes. Then hone in on your target until you see the results.

It could be a practical goal that you want to achieve, like losing a few pounds or saving up enough money for a trip to Europe. Perhaps it's a relationship-oriented goal, where you want to build bridges with a family member or find a new partner. You may want to work on aspects of your inner self that will help you to feel more confident and less anxious.

Whatever it is, by following the advice above, you will get the fifth piece of armor you need to make it happen. You may be wondering if you have the mental toughness to embark on such a life-changing journey and that's obviously a mindset that you need to develop if you want to see results. Even with the best will in the world, nothing can be achieved without a certain level of resilience: the powerful trait that enables you to manage and overcome any doubts or worries that may get in your way.

Mental toughness is the subject of our next chapter, and until then, I leave you with some inspiring words. Talking about his long career with the NBA, Michael Jordan stated,

---

"I've missed more than 9,000 shots in my career. I've lost almost 300 games. 26 times I've been trusted to take the game-winning shot and missed. I've failed over and over and over again in my life. And that is why I succeed."

— MICHAEL JORDAN

Now, let's get tough!

6

ARMOR PIECE 6 — MENTAL TOUGHNESS

ARE YOU A PUNCHING BAG OR A BOXER?

A punching bag is resilient. No matter how many times it is whacked by pounding fists, it will bounce back for more. That's why punching bags are made, but you wouldn't describe them as being mentally tough. A professional boxer, on the other hand, will keep throwing the punches even if they are exhausted, injured, and losing the match. They keep going because they believe that they can win. They are mentally tough.

That's the difference between "taking it" and "making it."

It's the difference between "bouncing back" and "moving forward."

In short, it's all about how well you deal with challenges in life and whether you see them as an opportunity for success or just another shot below the belt.

We all take knocks in life — some of them more serious than others — and can usually recover from them without too much damage. Your house may have been flooded after a torrential downpour or you might have lost your job — both potentially devastating events and requiring immediate action. Of course, you will need to set about getting your home back in order or look for work, because you don't have any other choice. But that doesn't necessarily mean that you are mentally tough.

What exactly is mental toughness then? This is a question we are going to look into and, once you get to the end of this chapter, you will have a clearer picture of how to develop it. We will also look at the difference between mental toughness and resilience and learn new strategies to combine both to your advantage. As the sixth piece of armor in your bodysuit, mental toughness is one of the main skills that you need to acquire if you want to get anywhere, and I would compare it to a helmet that protects your head because mental strength is cultivated in the mind.

Mental toughness

Our mind is like a muscle. The more we use it, the stronger it becomes. Just as you go to the gym to work on building up your body, gaining mental strength requires hard work and perseverance. You also need to get rid of bad habits that may be holding you back. Usually, we talk about athletes and elite special forces units when trying to explain mental toughness, as they seem to portray the perfect combo of physical prowess and mental strength. But we aren't all Super League players, world-class sprinters, or Olympic swimmers. Most of us are just ordinary folk, grappling with life in all of its complexities and trying to achieve our personal goals, whatever they may be.

Although I've mentioned a couple of world-class athletes in this book, the truth is that we are all involved in a long-distance run called life and have end goals that we want to reach. Mine is to motivate and coach others to get on a positive and healthy path, and I have laid out a detailed plan that I am following to achieve that. You may want to build up your business, leave your day job, get married, climb Pikes Peak in Colorado, or simply increase your overall sense of well-being. All noble pursuits require discipline, motivation, and vision. But more than that: you have to be mentally tough to manage any ups and downs along the way. If you crumble at the first setback, you won't get very far, so having the mental strength to continue is key.

In his research for the Department of Psychology at Manchester Metropolitan University, Peter Clough presented the definition of mental strength as:

> "the individual's capacity to effectively deal with stressors, pressures, and challenges and perform to the best of their ability, irrespective of the circumstances in which they find themselves."
>
> — PETER CLOUGH

We are all different and have our own characters, behaviors, and opinions. Despite that, we can all develop the mindset of mental toughness. Our mind is, after all, what we think at any given point, and it's well known today that we can control those thoughts. Your capacity to acquire a stronger mindset is totally feasible, which will then allow you to be more effective in handling stressful situations, external pressures, and challenges. No matter what situation you find yourself in, you can confront it with greater success than you might imagine.

I remember watching the brilliant movie *Unbroken* (2015), which recounts the life of Louis Zamperini, an Olympic runner who was taken prisoner by Japanese forces during World War II. As he narrates the story of his capture, torture, and eventual release, the main character states; "... my brother used to think that I could do anything... that I was better than I am..." His brother was right — Zamperini managed to overcome incredible physical and mental hardships before finally being rescued. If we can take anything from that movie, it's that we really don't know just how much we can take until our limits are stretched. As the protagonist said, "If I can take it, I can make it," and that's not only referring to resilience, but to the strength to believe in himself.

Hopefully, we don't need to go through what he did to build up our mental strength, but stories like this about the power of the human spirit are plenty. They can inspire us to overcome any challenge that we face as long as we understand what they are trying to teach us. When you say things like. "I don't think I can make it…," you are already allowing your mind to control your actions. The word "think" is your mind talking to you and it's defining what is or isn't possible without your consent. It's placing restrictions on you without your permission. Think about that!

Once you throw in the towel (another sporting term), you are done. You have given up, admitted defeat, and stopped trying anymore. That's self-sabotage, especially if there were other possibilities that you didn't explore or if you failed to look for reasons to keep going.

Why is having it so important?

Mental toughness is a learned skill, either through a conscious effort or as a result of life experiences. Assuming that it is something you want to acquire, here I'm referring to it as a skill you can learn that will bring benefits to all areas of your life. It's been noted that people with this "asset" seem to rise more easily than others to positions of leadership or authority and tend to excel in their personal lives. Acquiring this mindset is therefore critically important and valuable for everyone, and it can positively shape behavior.

All of the research shows that **mental toughness makes individuals perform better, deliver more results, show greater commitment, and be more competitive.** Perhaps you are wondering how that fits into your desire to achieve a personal goal, such as starting a small business, an online e-commerce store, or finding a new job. If you have tried starting up a new business or have applied for more jobs than you can remember without success, it is easy to slip into a pessimistic mindset. You will begin to tell yourself that you are NEVER going to build a successful business or find work, that no one thinks you are good enough, that you are useless… and so on. Eventually, you will stop pursuing that business venture, stop applying for jobs, or do so half-heartedly. Failing to give it your best shot, you will eventually give up. I can relate to that, but it doesn't have to be that way.

When I got home from my mission trip in 2012, I had no idea what I was going to do for work. My wife, who was my girlfriend at the time, was still in her own country continuing her education, but I was determined to make a life for us. So, I got a job as a window cleaning technician for a company in the prestigious Coachella Valley. It was a hard two years, but I embraced this line of work and learned all the minute technical details, logistics, marketing, and business side of the industry. I was on a new mission: to marry my wife and create a life for us, so I pushed through. After those two years, I parted ways with the company to start and operate my own window cleaning company, with less than $1,000 to my name. I used that money to buy an old white 2003 Chevrolet Silverado 1500 and worked incredibly hard to get my business off the ground.

As a business owner, you have to undergo a lot of hurdles to get to where you want to be and definitely need mental toughness to grow a successful business from nothing. Once you feel motivated though and have a plan, you can work through the challenges, always keeping your eye on the end goal.

A person with mental toughness will NEVER have those thoughts of failure or giving up. Instead, they will tell themselves that something will come up, that they are good enough, and that they have many skills and qualities to offer a prospective employer. They will prepare better, work harder, up-skill, and remain focused. And they will keep going, while you have stopped looking.

That isn't an impossible skill to achieve. It simply requires a shift in the way you think. Confidence in yourself is a key factor here and if you are still struggling with that issue, you need to go back to chapter 2 and start applying the strategies found there. It is super important to build up your self-confidence if you want to achieve anything in life, and believing in yourself is the basic foundation of any success story.

You probably won't be surprised if I tell you that **mentally tough people are also more content in their lives.** This is because they can manage stressful situations better and are less likely to develop mental health issues such as anxiety disorders or depression. They are the ones who enjoy a good night's sleep and aren't up until the early hours of the morning worrying about this or that. If you can learn to be mentally strong, you can begin to push through things you didn't think were possible and enjoy life more. It's as simple as that. When a stressful situation arises, you will be able to put things into perspective and see it as a challenge rather than as a crisis.

That's the difference in the mindset of someone with mental strength and someone without it: seeing life as being full of challenges, not crises.

When faced with what seems like an impossible task, the mentally tough will say, **"Yes, I can do that, or at least try,"** while others will run from the building. If their car breaks down on the highway, they will seek a solution and not curl up into a ball on the side of the road. It's all about seeing the positives rather than the negatives and this way of thinking solves problems. When the going gets tough, someone with that mental strength is more able to adjust to change, or at least be flexible enough to consider other options. You see, being mentally strong isn't about stubbornness or thinking that you know it all; it's got more to do with being adaptable under any circumstances.

Another trait that mentally tough people have is that **they set their sights high** and are more prepared to take risks. This doesn't mean a gung-ho approach, but involves being prepared to fail. Ouch! I know you probably hate that word, but guess what: mentally tough people aren't afraid of failure. They are afraid of not trying in the first place!

As I said earlier, resilience is something else. You can be resilient yet not particularly mentally tough. If you lack confidence and optimism, being resilient is not enough to get you where you want to be. I am not saying that resilience in itself is useless, but you can only be knocked down so many times before you stop getting up. A mentally strong person will not only get back up but will work on preventing themselves from being knocked down again because they believe that they can.

You may have experiences of being in a toxic relationship where you felt trapped, or have maintained a long-term partnership that you feel unhappy in. A resilient person will continue in either scenario to expect the worst. In a way, it's a kind of acceptance, with a mindset of, "this is just the way things are." Wrong! It takes two to be complicit in a relationship and although your perseverance is admirable, it is actually doing you more harm than good.

Someone who has the skills of mental toughness will find ways to actively change the dynamics of the relationship, and if that is not viable, will walk away from it. It's not about failure — it's about wise choices, having the guts to make a change and being prepared for any fallout. Those who continue to suffer may class themselves as resilient — being able to stand the situation. But this is a passive reaction as they don't feel that they have any power to change things. What they are saying is that they believe they have no choice, so they just have to take it like a man (or woman). On the other hand, someone with self-confidence will find ways to manage stress or pressure irrespective of the circumstances and has the mental strength to confront those challenges with a positive mindset. Whereas being resilient may help you to survive, it's mental toughness that will probably help you to succeed in life.

In other words, all mentally tough individuals are resilient, but not all resilient individuals are mentally tough.

If mental resilience is the means of adapting well in the face of adversity, trauma, tragedy, threats, or stress, then mental toughness is the ability to stay strong in the face of adversity, to keep focus and determination despite the difficulties. It's like the punching bag and the boxer that I talked about at the beginning of the chapter, and you need to decide which one you want to be.

Going back to Peter Clough and his work, he describes four important traits of mental toughness, which he calls the four C's. You may already have some of these traits but by acquiring all of them, you are more likely to achieve success. Let's take a quick look at what they are:

- Confidence
- Challenge
- Control
- Commitment

Confidence comes from discipline and training and isn't just about having a big idea of yourself. It comes down to BELIEVING in "you" and your ability to reach your goals. It also means not giving up when the road gets rocky and you need the right skillset to feel confident. Believing in yourself is the door to a world of possibilities.

Challenge is often a scary word for many, but for a mentally tough person, it's a case of, "Bring it on!" Got an important exam coming up? See it as an opportunity to show what you can do, rather than a terrifying experience that causes you to break out in a cold sweat. Whatever the outcome, pass or fail, life goes on and lessons can be learned. See challenges as a chance to grow and progress, rather than intimidating obstacles that you would rather not tackle.

Control what you can and leave what you can't. Stress can be a major factor when you attempt to micromanage things that are totally out of your control, leaving you feeling frustrated and impotent. Those with a mentally tough mindset focus on what is in their power to change and use confidence to see it through. They also believe that they are in control of their own lives and not at the mercy of external events or other people. This is a hard one to crack but by taking control of your life, you will see how this translates into better outcomes in the long run.

Commitment is the skill of sticking to your goals, no matter how many setbacks you come across on the way. Seeing failure as a speed bump and not the end of the world is something that you need to take on board because no matter what your goals are, you will have some failures and can't afford to let them stop you.

After my wife and I lost our son, I decided to sell the successful business I had worked so hard to build and enlisted in the U.S. Army as an 11B. Cleaning windows hadn't been something I was passionate about and, after our tragic loss, it was time to really reflect on where I was in life. To be honest, I didn't feel happy with where I was at the time. My business had been a means to an end, not something that fulfilled me. So I had to let it go, as difficult as that was, considering all of the effort I had put into establishing it, but my mind was made up.

Going through the 22-week O.S.U.T. (One Station Unit Training) during the COVID-19 pandemic was not an easy process, especially as a 30-year-old man. It was both mentally and physically challenging even while I was one of the fittest guys in my platoon. However, through the military, I found that I aspired to coach people through life and business, which has led me to the creation of this book. Joining the infantry was a way of processing the loss of my son. I needed time to heal so I could move forward and identify what I am truly passionate about. I had to place myself in an uncomfortable environment to be completely real with myself and face who I am. I understand that it is hard to be mentally tough when going through a bad situation that you don't quite understand or can't control. I really do. But I will tell you that no matter what you are unexpectedly hit with in life, you can find the strength to carry on with a tough mind and a resilient heart. Sometimes that means stepping outside of your comfort zone or sacrificing things that you once thought were important to you. This can give you space to reassess your priorities and give you the strength to work towards a better future.

From your personal life to your professional career, using the four C's is a good place to begin thinking about mental toughness. I have some other strategies for you to follow and as you begin to master each one, you will start to see life from a whole new perspective. Remember that mental toughness begins in the way you think about things and what your mind is telling you. Now it's time to take control of that narrative as you create a new dialogue for success.

Cultivating Mental Toughness

1. Positive self-talk

U.S. Navy SEALs go through rigorous training to help them develop a fearless mindset. One of the exercises involves trainees being held underwater without oxygen for a long period. Instead of listening to their inner voice, which tells them that they are going to die, they learn to work through the panic by telling themselves that they will survive. Positive self-talk is an extremely powerful skill that you should use if you want to be mentally strong, and you don't have to be a Navy SEAL to do it. Throughout each day, keep talking to yourself in the second person and be your own coach. Say things like, "You are going to give this your best shot, you can do it." This kind of positive self-talk will have you ready to go and believing in your capabilities.

2. Set goals

Take the time to write down what your goals are or what you aim to achieve and make a daily check from now on of how well you are doing. Each goal can have a specific milestone, which can be big or small. What matters is that you set yourself something to do each day, which will get you into the habit of being focused on achieving the ultimate end goal. Think of it as a personal daily workout for your mind and use your time wisely, even if it's only five minutes a day. Track your progress and when you achieve each goal, set yourself a new one. By staying in a constant state of achievement, you will feel more positive and optimistic about your chances of success.

3. Visualize

Every time you visualize your hand on the prize, you are forming an image in your brain of a projected possibility. When you do so, your brain begins to believe it is a done deal and starts preparing for the victory run. All athletes use this strategy to help them succeed and it's also a very important tactical skill used by the armed forces. Through mental rehearsal, you can even visualize possible problems in the future and thus be more mentally prepared for them if they show up.

4. Simulate

There's a very good reason why professional pilots do a lot of their training on simulators, in which real flight conditions are created. But you can practice this technique too and go through the motions of a future scenario to be better mentally prepared for it. Want to get that new business off the ground and need to talk to your bank manager about a loan? Write down your business plan and act out the scene with another colleague or friend. This will enable you to be ready for anything that comes up in the conversation and, hopefully, has you leaving the meeting with a loan secured in your account.

5. Find your motivation

If the motivation doesn't come from within you, you have less chance of succeeding. Why? Because you are trying to do something for all the wrong reasons, expressing doubt about your abilities, and you are more likely to quit because of that. When you aim for something for your own sake or for loved ones, you will experience more drive and determination to move forward. It's not about focusing on the rewards either, but rather gaining satisfaction from overcoming the challenge. A pat on the back or shiny trophy is great, but it's intrinsic motivation that will keep you in the race.

6. Stay true to your values

Your values are important, and if you don't know what they are, it may be difficult to stay on track with your goals. Your deep, inner beliefs form part of your value system and can be anything from your faith to strongly-held views on the environment. When you live according to your value system, you are more likely to have direction and be spurred on to keep going. Make sure when you set out to achieve anything that your values are reflected and stay as close to them as you can.

7. Overcoming setbacks

Imagine if a sprinter in the 400-meter hurdles panicked every time he saw a hurdle in front of him — there would be absolutely no point in competing at all! Life is like that — full of obstacles, challenges, failures — whatever you want to call them. It's all about how you bounce back and keep going with a renewed sense of vigor and determination. Not only that, it is OK to fail now and again because it makes you learn new ways of coping and go on to excel in the future. Don't fear failure!

8. Controlled exposure

By exposing yourself gradually to situations that may provoke anxiety, you can learn to overcome your fears. Similar to how someone with arachnophobia is encouraged to look at a picture of a spider to reduce their fear, you can try taking yourself out of your comfort zone a bit at a time and get used to working on whatever is making you feel stressed. Test the water until your mind learns that there is nothing to fear and nurture self-confidence in your abilities as you do so.

9. Strength through unity

Very often, people feel that they are alone in whatever it is they are going through, which can be psychologically debilitating. Having someone to share your worries or triumphs with is important and that could be anyone, from your spouse or business partner to friends and family. No one achieves anything completely by themselves and we all depend on others, whether we are aware of it or not. Having someone to back you up will help you to go on, and if no one seems suitable in your circle, find a mentor or join a peer group. Asking for support or help doesn't make you weak. It makes you brave and bold!

10. Stop the hate

Hate is a very destructive emotion that is often fueled by distorted thought processes, and the main person it damages is you. It can build up inside if not dealt with and cause you to have a warped view of reality. Don't forget that each time we feel an intense emotion like hate, we are using up a lot of energy that could be better spent else-where. In addition, it can have adverse effects on your physical well-being, causing stress levels to rise as well as headaches, digestive problems, inflammation, and attacks on your immune system. Try practicing empathy and compassion for your fellow human beings, establish your boundaries, and stop letting negative emotions such as hate and anger impact your life.

11. Working through conflict

Conflict can arise at any time and is a completely unavoidable part of life. What matters is how you take it on and it can go one of two ways: 1. either you get embroiled emotionally and come out feeling wounded and hurt, or 2. you aim to resolve any differences in a healthy manner, build trust and understanding, and strengthen your relationships. Which one do you prefer? I hope you said 2, and the way to achieve that is by practicing emotional intelligence. This means getting in touch with your feelings, communicating them clearly, and understanding where the other person is coming from. You should also aim to stay calm, be able to interpret both verbal and nonverbal communication, and respect differences.

Let's just finish here by saying that stress is a very dangerous reaction to any conflict situation as things can easily spiral out of control. Not only that, nothing is ever resolved by confrontational anger and it certainly won't benefit you in any way. Learning to relieve stress before it builds up will allow you to stay balanced and focused, preventing irrational emotions and reactions from coming into play. For your well-being and peace of mind, always look for resolutions rather than focusing on "being right." It's not about who wins or loses, so shift your mindset of wanting to come out on top all the time. This takes grace and humility, but it is also a skill of mental toughness as you learn to choose your battles and save your energy for things worth fighting for.

Having emotional intelligence is a skill that can be extremely useful in all aspects of our lives, not just for mental strength. You can learn more about it in the next chapter and it's the last piece of our armor in your full body suit of resilience and tunnel-vision focus! Here's a taste of what we will be discussing, with a quote by the Austrian neurologist, psychiatrist, philosopher, author, and Holocaust survivor, Victor E. Frankl:

"Between stimulus and response, there is a space. In that space lies our freedom and power to choose our response. In our response lies our growth and freedom."

— VICTOR E. FRANKL

Time to tackle those emotions!

7

ARMOR PIECE 7 — EMOTIONAL RESILIENCE

HOW DO YOU REACT WHEN FACED WITH A STRESSFUL SITUATION?

D o you panic, get angry, or shut down altogether?

Usually, these kinds of reactions do more harm than good and certainly don't help you to work through what is happening to find a solution. It may seem natural to become irritated when you feel under pressure or let off steam by ranting and raving if things take an unexpected turn. Closing in on yourself is also an option taken by many, although none of these behaviors lead to any positive results. They are the hallmark of people who aren't handling themselves well and this is because they haven't cultivated emotional resilience. This term is used when describing people who react more positively to stressful situations and cope with them in a healthy and constructive way.

As you know by now, stress is a response that is triggered in our brain when we feel threatened or in danger, and is a throwback to our archaic survival instinct. Most of the time, we overreact and that induces physical symptoms as well as affecting our ability to think or act clearly. But some situations in life really do warrant stress, which we can either use to spur us on or allow it to destroy us. I want to help you cultivate the former response.

To do this, you need to have three things: **self-belief, self-compassion,** and **enhanced cognition.** These are the three superpowers that will enable you to see adversities as "temporary" and keep learning from the pain and suffering that you might feel. As the final piece of armor in your bodysuit, emotional resilience is a trait that you probably haven't thought too much about before now.

It's likely that you haven't considered your emotional responses to everyday events and relationships with others, and may even contest that you are always justified in acting the way you do. It could be that you think shouting is normal and getting all worked up is an acceptable response when you are under pressure. But what if I told you that these responses are counterproductive to your well-being and usually don't bring you the best outcome?

How you react to trauma, tragedy, or other life stress is a mixture of learned behavior and choices. Although building emotional resilience tends to start from a young age, you can cultivate it through experiences later in life. If you were brought up by parents who gave you the time and space to figure things out for yourself, instead of spoon-feeding you with ready solutions, then you will have acquired a certain amount of emotional resilience. If not, there is still time to learn.

When I was growing up, I wasn't very good at dealing with my emotions and kept a lot of my anger locked inside me. Whenever I faced one of life's hurdles, frustration got buried along with everything else. The tragic death of my newborn son in 2019 and the near-loss of my wife brought me to the point where I seriously needed to confront how I was feeling. It was one of those dramatic moments in life when I realized that I had to find a way to get through this terrible experience, not only for my sake but also for hers.

It began when my wife was feeling so unwell in the 20th week of her pregnancy that I decided to take her to see the doctor; and when we got there, we were immediately sent to a hospital across the street for emergency treatment. After taking her blood pressure and doing some blood work, we found out that her blood pressure was so high that she would have to be admitted in order to stabilize her.

The tests showed that she was suffering from severe preeclampsia, something that is quite uncommon and only affects 5 to 8% of all pregnancies. The worst news of all was that, due to the dangerous condition that she was in, the doctors told us we needed to abort our son immediately. I don't know if you can imagine how we felt when we were told that. But we were both adamant that no way was this going to happen and insisted that the team do everything in their powers to keep our son alive. They were then forced to direct us to another hospital that specialized in complicated pregnancies and neonatal care to treat my wife.

To cut a long story short, my son was 20 weeks old and my wife and I fought for about a week and a half to keep him alive. As the days went by, even more complications set in and my wife's health was plummeting due to very high blood pressure. After a few days, the doctors told us the blood circulation had stopped and that our son wasn't growing the way he was supposed to. By now, my wife was prepared to die to keep our son alive and I did a lot of praying during that intensely fraught time, accompanied by my friends and family.

Fortunately, she did begin to stabilize and was moved out of the ER into a room of her own, where she should have stayed for the rest of the pregnancy. However, my wife's blood pressure skyrocketed again after a few days, causing her liver and kidneys to start failing rapidly. The blood stopped circulating through my son completely and she was heavily drugged to keep her stabilized and avoid the possibility of having a stroke.

I couldn't communicate with her and have never felt more alone in my life. The final decision weighed heavily on my shoulders alone and it was a predicament that I could never have planned for. The doctors informed me that my son would not make it and, if we kept on going like this, I would lose my wife too. Needless to say, this was the hardest decision I ever had to make in my entire life, and it wasn't about me. It was about my wife and son. I cried and asked God, "*Why?*"

> *Why would God put me in this position?*
> *I didn't want to make this decision.*
> *I didn't want to have to choose one or the other, even though the fate of my son was sealed.*
> *I couldn't choose lives for both my son and my wife, whom I loved equally.*
> *Why, why, why...?*

I was screaming inside and felt desperate, angry, and confused. But I had to finally make that decision: we were going to give birth to our 21-week-old son to keep my wife alive. She was induced and gave birth naturally but when they pulled my son out, he didn't have any pulse. We assume that he died during labor, although we did get to hold little Elijah Alexander and see his beautiful tiny nose, hands, and feet. He was so perfect, but eventually, we had to say goodbye to him.

Now, we know he is in a better place and we choose to stay positive, moving forward with optimism as a couple, with our faith stronger than ever. As I recall those moments of despair, I realize the intense emotions were natural, but I couldn't let them destroy me. I had to overcome them to be able to make a rational decision and to take responsibility for two lives. It was a turning point for me and, although I would never wish for anyone to have to go through the same thing, I believe it helped me to grow.

Since then, I approach adversity differently and don't see every setback as a permanent block. Instead of panicking, I focus on finding solutions and don't let anxiety overtake my thinking. It's a fine balance, but one that I have learned to master and, although nothing can be gained from the loss of a loved one, it can help you to understand the grief of others and to support them. That is the beauty of emotional resilience, which also allows you to have compassion, empathy, and understanding for others.

When you learn to be more emotionally resilient, you can enjoy a much healthier, more mature, and optimistic approach to life. You are better equipped to cope with stress, tragedy, or any setbacks that come your way. This means managing your emotions and reactions effectively, rather than having a panic attack or shutting down any feelings at all. There is a middle ground, where you can feel and still act wisely in the face of negative circumstances. By all means, vent how you feel, but don't let those intensely negative emotions be the driving force behind your actions.

People who practice emotional resilience feel just as intensely as you or I, but they also see the silver lining or at least can reframe their perspective from one of doom and gloom to positivity and hope. You don't need to go through a life-changing tragedy to get to that point (and I hope that you never do), but it is a skill that can be learned at any moment of the day in a variety of ways.

Emotional resilience is the light at the end of the tunnel, the ray of sunshine behind the clouds, and the hope for a better future. When you approach setbacks in this way, you are much more likely to sail through the storm and come out unscathed.

If you have had negative experiences in the past, it is useful to remember that what you went through has given you the wisdom that you have today, and any problems you face now will bring you more wisdom in the future.

DEVELOPING EMOTIONAL RESILIENCE

You can learn to adapt to stressful situations or crises and come out of them without any lasting impact on your well-being. Those who are emotionally resilient have less trouble confronting stress and life changes, so it is definitely a skill that you should have in your arsenal. It also protects your mental and physical health and can prevent chronic illnesses associated with stress such as obesity, diabetes, gastrointestinal conditions, heart disease, anxiety disorders, and premature death.

The only thing that distinguishes a resilient from a non-resilient person is the way the former chooses to respond. Having emotional resilience doesn't mean that they aren't affected by stress or won't get upset. It simply allows them to keep getting up when knocked back, and not be put off by negativity or pessimism. Instead of getting overwhelmed by their emotions, they continue, despite the setbacks.

As I mentioned earlier in this chapter, **self-belief, self-compassion** and **enhanced cognition** are three tools that will help you to be successful.

Self-belief is about recognizing your strengths and weaknesses and using them to your advantage. Be the person to say, "I don't know how to do this task, but I will learn," rather than the one who says, "I'm useless at this and will never succeed."

Self-compassion means being kind to yourself, just in the same way that you would be to others. Forgive your mistakes and don't wallow in self-pity, because that is not going to take you anywhere. Instead, accept your faults or mistakes and don't think any less of yourself. When you nurture your needs, you will create a greater sense of self-worth and positivity.

Enhanced cognition is related to the way we think. By being more aware of our self-sabotaging thoughts, it is possible to get them under control and prevent them from causing chaos. Our thoughts can be used to analyze and evaluate situations objectively, which then leads to actions that are more productive and less reactive.

If you want to begin to nurture your emotional resilience, you need to:

- Recognize that your thoughts influence your actions
- Acknowledge stress and be willing to cope with it effectively
- Be open to changes and ready to adapt to new situations
- Accept that changing the way you react to stress can make a difference
- Embrace self-compassion and empathy

That doesn't sound too difficult, does it?

Think of all the things that have happened to you in the past, and what long-term effects they had on your life. You may have made bad relationship choices, kept company with friends who were a bad influence on you, or failed to qualify for your chosen career. How you dealt with those instances then has a direct correlation with how you are feeling now. Being aware of that is a very good starting point from which to evaluate what you can do better next time, and how you can overcome similar predicaments.

Are you emotionally resilient?

I want you to focus on yourself and answer the questions below, from which you can gain some insight into how emotionally resilient you are. There are no right or wrong answers, so you don't need to feel stressed. This is a small exercise in self-reflection, not a test of your character, so be easy on yourself and answer honestly.

Reply by giving yourself a number on a scale of **1 to 5**:

1 = never
2 = rarely
3 = sometimes
4 = often
5 = always

Let's see how you do:

	1	2	3	4	5
1. Are you aware of your thoughts, emotions, and inner potential?					
2. Do you think before you react?					
3. Are you patient, understanding, and willing to adapt?					
4. Do you practice acceptance and forgiveness?					
5. Do you focus on finding solutions?					
6. Do you express your emotions in a socially acceptable manner?					
7. Do you bottle up negative emotions?					
8. Can you create and sustain long-term relationships?					
9. Are you ashamed to ask for help when you need it?					
10. Do you like to resolve conflicts in discussions?					

Once you have thought about the questions, you may find that you answer **never** to some, or **always** to others. What matters here is to focus on any areas that you would like to improve on. Acknowledging that is the first step in changing whatever you are dissatisfied with. When you discover what aspects of your thoughts are preventing you from leading a happier, more content life, that can be a game-changer.

If you are brave enough, you can also pose these same questions to a close friend or loved one, asking them to answer about you. For example, ask them how aware of your thoughts, emotions, and inner potential you appear to be to them. You may be surprised at their answers, and it is something that can give you even greater perspective.

Building emotional resilience

In all spheres of our life we may experience stressful situations, tragedies, traumas, or conflicts. How we react to them can affect our physical and mental health. The key here is to work with your emotions so that they do not add fuel to the fire. You may need to venture out of your comfort zone here and readjust to a different kind of behavior pattern.

I would like to emphasize that I don't want you to do anything here that doesn't feel right to you or which goes against your belief system and values. The point isn't to sacrifice what is important to you or feel that you need to change your personality, beliefs, or views. You can and should continue to be who you are and not bury any strong emotions that arise. Go about your life as normal, with the added tool of stopping now and again to be more mindful of what is going on inside your head.

Emotions are, after all, part of being human and we experience them for a reason. They aren't your enemy, but knowing how to act when such strong feelings come to the fore will lead you to a much better outcome than one ruled by emotional impulses and over-reactions. Remember too that mental toughness comes from having compassion for yourself and empathy for others. If you hold a position of leadership, being mentally tough doesn't mean ignoring or running roughshod over other people's emotions, but having insight into your own emotions and those of others.

As a mentor and coach, I often get to hear stories from people who have suffered a loss, gone through trauma, or are facing difficulties in life. One thing that is important to me is to be able to empathize with their situation, but not allow their painful negative emotions to overwhelm me. In other words, I don't put myself in a position where I sacrifice my own sense of well-being by taking on the problems of others. I can support that person without necessarily feeling the same emotions because I am seeing it from an outside perspective.

This doesn't mean that I care any less; but by maintaining that non-emotional perspective, I am in a much better position to help the other person in a clear, objective way. This is a technique that you can begin to practice on yourself, by stepping out of the "you" for a moment and visualizing that you are an observer to what is going on, rather than a participant. It takes some discipline, but once you get the hang of it, you will stop feeling caught up in a tornado every time you experience strong emotions.

HERE ARE MY TOP TEN TECHNIQUES TO BEGIN BUILDING YOUR EMOTIONAL RESILIENCE:

1. Notice emerging emotions

Simply by observing that you are feeling upset about something, you can process the emotions in healthier ways. The next time someone upsets you, instead of going ballistic and swearing at them, confront them with compassion, and if that isn't possible, set clear boundaries about what you find acceptable or unacceptable.

2. Modify self-judgment

Tune in to your inner critic and turn down the volume when you hear it castigating you. Better still, switch the channel to one where the only voice you hear is that of self-love and compassion. Ask yourself, "If someone else talked to me like this, how would I respond?" Hopefully, your answer will give you great insight into how damaging your inner critic can be.

3. Be curious

Often, we become aware of negative emotions and get swept along by them, without stopping to find out what is really causing them. By being curious about your thoughts, behavior, and emotions, you can begin to have more understanding of what triggers them and how to process them. Simply ask yourself, "Why am I feeling this way? What is making me react like this? What makes it so important?"

4. Practice emotional regulation

Emotions are healthy responses to life as we experience it, but when they become overpowering, they can lead us to make the wrong choices. Having a coping strategy will enable you to respond to any situation calmly without things getting out of control. Some of these strategies include meditation, listening to music, journaling, or even talking to a professional therapist.

- By meditating for even ten minutes per day, you are allowing yourself to be calm and still, instead of agitated and upset.
- Listening to calming music affects the frequency of our brain waves and slows down our pulse. It helps the autonomic nervous system to recover faster and reduces the endocrine and psychological stress response. And it's a great way to take your mind off whatever is bothering you.
- When you keep a journal, you are relieving yourself of all the weight that you are carrying around in your head. It is also really useful to read what you have written, because when you see

things in black and white, they will become clearer.

- Many excellent therapists are available to help you to work through your emotions and guide you in how to cope with them. Being impartial, a therapist can listen to you without judgment or criticism and provide you with self-help strategies to aid your journey to well-being.

5. Exercise regularly

Physical exercise is a wonderful de-stressor and also nourishes your emotional health, leaving you feeling strong and positive. With just 30 minutes a day set aside for some kind of physical activity, you will immediately notice the benefits. Begin your workout or run in an angry mood and notice how all of that negative emotion dissipates by the end, leaving you wondering what you were angry about in the first place.

6. Strengthen social connections

It can be very hard to cope with difficult situations on your own and loneliness can seriously impact your mental health. For that reason, try to stay connected with your loved ones and nurture those bonds as much as possible. Whether it be by email, a quick phone call, or a video chat, stay in touch with those you care about and allow them to be at your side if you need them.

7. Practice mindfulness

There is a lot of new research linking mindfulness with less emotional reactivity and it is something that can be done anytime, anywhere. Although there are various methods, it all comes down to being present at any given moment. This means stopping to take in your surroundings, state of mind, any thoughts or emotions, and simply observe them. You can progress to guided meditation or visualization sessions if you like, all of which are known to make us more aware of ourselves and help to bring inner balance.

8. Cultivate optimism

Whenever you read or hear about truly resilient people who have gone through extreme hardships or survived life-threatening situations, they all have one thing in common: positivity. This is balanced by realism and isn't some rose-tinted view of the world, but it has proved essential in helping them to achieve their goals. Although you should pay attention to the negatives, learn not to focus on them and concentrate instead on problems that can be solved. Also, believe in yourself and your capabilities to win through.

9. Have a moral compass

Sit down and think about your values — what you hold to be right and wrong, good and true, and stick to them, no matter what. When a crisis emerges to test you, you can use your moral compass as a guide to help you respond in a way that truly represents you. Altruism, selflessness, kindness, and compassion are just some of the points on your moral compass that you can use to steer you through life and fortify your sense of direction when feeling lost or overwhelmed.

10. Use cognitive flexibility

You may be wondering what that is exactly. It basically comes down to being flexible about how you view challenges and the way you react to stress. One good example is to inject more humor into your life — it can be a powerful coping mechanism that allows you to reduce stress and build resilience. Laughter is very useful because it helps you to put things into perspective and to take a step back from whatever is causing you stress. Having that flexibility allows you to find new ways of overcoming challenges without wear and tear to your nervous system.

One last approach that I want to talk about concerning emotional resilience is a method called **"Flip the Switch."** It's a relatively new way of dealing with the issue and involves switching off stress chemicals and activating a surge of healing chemicals. It may sound difficult to achieve, but with a little practice, you can do it. The technique is based on the notion that we can get the brain to see stress as a positive experience, rather than a negative one. Think of it as rewiring how we usually respond to stress with a little tweaking here and there. When stimuli arrive in the brain, there is a circuit board of nerves that tells us how to feel, what to expect, and how to respond.

Chemical and electrical responses are then fired, without us even having to think about what is going on.

We can react in one of two ways: with resiliency or reactivity. Stress can either incite us to be resilient or trigger extreme reactions that also activate other stress circuits. When in resilience mode, the executive functioning of our brain (logic, rationale, problem-solving) remains intact; but in stress mode, that feature is disabled and becomes unresponsive. This is when we need tools to switch off emotional circuits and to reduce the levels of stress that we experience and maintain control.

To do this, we need to begin with a moment of mindfulness, which then turns into the processing of emotions. It is important to let that emotion have its voice, let's say anger, and as we observe it, we will notice that it then subsides. Mindfulness allows the executive function to stay enabled and as the negative emotions come and go, they eventually give way to positive feelings.

Flipping the switch is an easy technique, once you understand how it works, and it is something that will definitely be of use to you. Here's how you can apply it in any situation:

Step 1

Stop and observe your emotions of anger, sadness, jealousy, or other negative urges. Acknowledge that your emotions may be leading you to make a wrong decision or bad action.

Step 2

Imagine that there is a switch somewhere on your body or within you. It could be on your head, chest, hand, or inside your brain. Whenever you flip this switch, all your emotions are rerouted, and all your decision-making abilities are redirected to the logic part of your brain. I want you to actually visualize the switch and literally flip it!

Step 3

No matter where that switch is on your body, or even in your brain, actually go through the motion of switching it off with your hand. You are flipping those emotions, sending them off into another direction so that the executive part of your brain can function undistracted.

Step 4

Now you can redress the situation using the logical part of your brain and make the best decision based on facts and rationale rather than emotional highs or lows. It's as simple as this: feel angry, notice your anger, flip the switch to send it elsewhere, and now use your logic to handle whatever triggered that emotion. Done!

Most of the time, it is very easy to get carried away by our emotions, without stopping to think about what damage they are doing. How often have you regretted your behavior during a temper tantrum or a bout of anger? The results can often be catastrophic — both for you and those around you.

When you can master emotional resilience, you will be better equipped to manage your personal life, social life, and the experience of life itself. This is an amazing piece of armor for your mind and one which liberates you from negative feelings.

With a toolkit of self-acceptance, empathy, and reasoning, you can achieve better emotional regulation, which is the key to building emotional resilience and strength.

I'll end this chapter with one of the many quotes by a seminal figure in psychology who recognized the importance of resilience to well-being. Professor Michael Rutter, Professor of Developmental Psychopathology at King's College, London, said:

> *"Resilience can be defined as reduced vulnerability to environmental risk experiences, the overcoming of a stress or adversity, or a relatively good outcome despite risk experiences."*
>
> — PROFESSOR MICHAEL RUTTER

Now it's up to you to go for it!

CONCLUSION

About 3,400 years ago, someone in ancient Greece came up with the great idea of using bronze to make plate armor that protected the chest, back, neck, shoulders, upper arms, and upper legs of the soldiers. Bronze helmets and reinforced wooden shields soon followed. Up until then, the troops had relied on hardened cloth and leather to protect them from bladed weapons. As more powerful weapons were developed, the armor had to get tougher too. Through constant innovation and the introduction of new materials and techniques, warfare changed from one brutal battle to the next.

That's a real-life example of our resilience in the face of crisis and a wonderful metaphor for what I wanted to achieve with this book. You see, we may have been talking about mental resilience and conquering your ambitions, but it all began thousands of years ago when we realized that we needed to adapt to oncoming threats if we wanted to survive. Life can often feel like a battlefield, where you are constantly bombarded with challenges that can harm your mental well-being and it's up to you to protect yourself from that.

When you have the right mental armor, you can successfully manage any circumstances that test you and go on to pursue your goals full of positivity.

And here's the key takeaway that I want to stress: **You are your own worst enemy.**

- When you allow other people or situations to affect you, you are literally taking off your breastplate and exposing yourself to harm.
- When you beat yourself up about something you did or didn't do, you are removing your helmet and open to failure.
- When you get into a negative mode of thinking, you are vulnerable to any kind of attack.

It's up to you to arm yourself so that you can be a winner in life, no matter how difficult your past has been or how testing your future. That's what this book is about and I hope that you use every piece of body armor to build yourself more mental resilience, confidence, and happiness.

I've been through so much in my life, starting from a very young age when my mom was diagnosed with schizophrenia. I was the victim of sexual abuse, bullied a lot at school, and suffered from extremely low self-esteem. That was quite a lot for anyone to handle, and it would have been easy for me to end up in a very dark place. But, at some point, I had to take a good look at myself and see who I really was, and how I wanted to live my life. This was when I shifted my mindset and moved from negative thoughts to empowering ones. And you can do that too.

In this book, you will have found strategies for mastering the power of positive thinking, building unshakeable self-confidence, and establishing good habits. You will have identified a plan of action for shaking off the victim mentality, developing situational awareness, and tunnel-vision focus. You will have discovered the art of mental toughness and emotional resilience, both of which can help you to find greater fulfillment in all spheres of your life.

On a final note, I want to share a couple of personal insights with you:

- One valuable lesson that I have learned over the years is to never compare myself with others.
- A long time ago I also stopped questioning whether I am good enough, strong enough, capable enough.
- I have removed phrases like, "What if…," from my dictionary and stopped imagining the worst-case scenario for every single situation.

Bad things have happened, sure, and they will continue to do so. Losing my newborn child was probably the worst of them all, but life goes on. How you handle such events is entirely up to you, and you can either wallow in self-pity and inertia or grow from that and move on.

As George Washington, first President of the United States once said,

---

"The harder the conflict, the greater the triumph."

— GEORGE WASHINGTON

I hope that by developing your mental armor, you will begin today to take action and never give up. Don't surrender to life, but embrace it with all your heart, using the power that is within you to achieve all of your hopes and dreams.

Be strong, be resilient, stay focused, and conquer your ambitions with confidence.

You can do it!

LEAVE A REVIEW!

Word of mouth is such a powerful thing... Just one conversation can change your life forever.

As you know by now, I'm passionate about sharing knowledge and helping people in any way I can, and I know my book, *Armor Your Mind*, has the power to do that. The thing is, when you look up a subject on Amazon, the things you come across are the things with the most reviews... and **that's where you come in.**

If you could spare just a couple of minutes to share your honest review of *Armor Your Mind* on Amazon, this would help my book reach the readers who are looking for it - the people who really need it.

Accept Your **FREE Gift,** a Copy of **THE RULE OF 8!**

You are about to be one step closer to a healthier, happier, more fulfilled you!

In just a minute, you'll be able to access your FREE copy of **The Rule of 8,** a guide that will help you achieve the work/life balance you've always wanted.

Learn how to get the most out of a 24 hour day by managing your time in the most efficient way possible. After spending **years** feeling frazzled, burnt out, and unfulfilled, you can now maximize your health, sense of contentment, and even productivity by following the instructions in this simple, easy to read ebook.

Visit the link below to get a free PDF of **The Rule of 8** and start following it **today**!

WWW.THERULEOF8GUIDE.COM

SOURCES

https://www.apa.org/pubs/journals/
releases/bul-1316803.pdf

Lyubomirsky, S., King, L. (2005). "The Benefits of Frequent Positive Affect: Does Happiness Lead to Success?" *Psychological Bulletin*, American Psychological Association 2005, Vol. 131, No. 6, 803– 855.

https://www.apa.org/pubs/journals/
releases/bul-1304601.pdf

Segerstrom, S.C., Miller, G.E. (2004). "Psychological Stress and the Human Immune System: A Meta-Analytic Study of 30 Years of Inquiry University of British Columbia." *Psychological Bulletin*, American Psychological Association 2004, Vol. 130, No. 4, 601–630.

https://www.apa.org/pubs/journals/releases/
psp805804.pdf

Danner, D.D., Friesen W.V. (2001). "Positive Emotions in Early Life and Longevity: Findings from the *Nun Study*." *Journal of Personality and Social Psychology*, 2001, Vol. 80, No. 5, 804–813.

https://ppc.sas.upenn.edu/research/resilience-children

Gillham, J., Reivich, K., Seligman, M.E.P. (2007). "Resilience in Children." *University of Pennsylvania*.

https://www.sciencedirect.com/science/article/pii/S0005796715300814

Eagleson, C., Hayes, S., Mathews, A., Perman, G., Hirsch, C.R. (2016). "The power of positive thinking: Pathological worry is reduced by thought replacement in Generalized Anxiety Disorder." *Behaviour Research and Therapy*, Volume 78, Pages 13–18.

https://psycnet.apa.org/record/1988-26559-001

Scheier, M. F., & Carver, C. S. (1987). "Dispositional optimism and physical well-being: The influence of generalized outcome expectancies on health." *Journal of Personality*, 55(2), 169–210.

https://www.semanticscholar.org/paper/Positive-Thinking-in-Coping-with-Stress-and-Health-Naseem-Khalid/db77200dc777353a922594e868554b12e0c8448b

Naseem, Z, Khalid, R, (2010). "Positive Thinking in Coping with Stress and Health Outcomes: Literature Review."

https://www.semanticscholar.org/paper/Positive-psychology.-An-introduction.-Seligman-Csikszentmihalyi/6d8ba92034df85cc932f8faea39507bd5 8f481c8

Seligman, M, Csíkszentmihályi, M., (2000). "Positive psychology. An introduction." *American Psychologist* 55 1): 5–14.

https://lsme.ac.uk/blog/confidence-a-great-attribute-and-a-key-factor-in-the-realisation-of-your-goals

Skenderis, V. M. (2015). "Implementing a team approach to improve positive behavioral changes for 9th graders: An action research study." *Capella University*, ProQuest Information & Learning.

https://academic.oup.com/her/article/19/4/357/560320

Mann, M., Hosman, C. M. H., Schaalma, H. P., & de Vries, N. K. (2004). "Self-esteem in a broad-spectrum approach for mental health promotion." *Health Education Research*, 19, 357–372

https://psycnet.apa.org/record/1999-13171-003

Kramer, R. M. (1998). "Paranoid cognition in social systems: Thinking and acting in the shadow of doubt." *Personality and Social Psychology Review*, 4, 251–275

https://rdcu.be/ciPi6

Yang, J., Xu, X., Chen, Y. *et al.* (2016). "Trait self-esteem and neural activities related to self-evaluation and social feedback." *Scientific Reports* 6, 20274.

https://pubmed.ncbi.nlm.nih.gov/27452914/

Svedberg P, Hallsten L, Narusyte J, Bodin L, Blom V. (2016). "Genetic and environmental influences on the association between performance-based self-esteem and exhaustion: A study of the self-worth notion of burnout." *Scandinavian Journal of Psychology.* Oct;57(5):419–26. doi: 10.1111/sjop.12309. Epub 2016 Jul 25. PMID: 27452914.

https://journals.sagepub.com/doi/abs/10.1177/0956797610371963

Quoidbach, J., Dunn, E.W., Petrides, K.V., Mikolajczak, M. (2010). "Money Giveth, Money Taketh Away: The Dual Effect of Wealth on Happiness." *Psychological Science.* 21(6):759–763. doi:10.1177/0956797610371963.

https://www.scirp.org/(S(czeh2tfqy-w2orz553k1w0r45))/reference/ReferencesPapers.aspx?ReferenceID=1902775

Clough, P., Earle, K., Sewell, D. (2002). "Mental toughness: The concept and its measurement." *Solutions in sport psychology.* 32–46.

https://positivepsychology.com/mentally-strong/

Ribeiro, M. (2021). "How to Become Mentally Strong: 14 Strategies for Building Resilience" *Positive Psychology.com.*

Clough, P., Strycharczyk, D. (2015). *Developing Mental Toughness: Coaching Strategies to Improve Performance, Resilience and Wellbeing*, Second Edition. Kogan Page.

ACKNOWLEDGMENTS

I want to thank:

My beautiful wife, for her unwavering love and support, and for always believing in me.
My son, Elijah Alexander, who will always be in my heart.
My dad, for being a great example of what a hard worker and provider is.
My mom, for her contagious joy, compassion, and positivity.

My sisters, for making it through our childhood together with so many wonderful memories along the way.
Greg & LaDena, for taking me under their wing, mentoring me, and always feeding me.
Jeremy & Kim, for being incredible friends throughout the years and introducing me to real barbecue.

The Rivera family, for taking me into their home with open arms in my senior year so I could finish wrestling season.

I want to thank each and every person that has ever exuded positivity into my life, for speaking life into me, and to anyone that has ever taught me something.

Most of all, I want to thank God because without Him, I would not know how to love or receive it. Without Him, none of this would have been possible.

About the Author

Carl Prox is a dedicated life coach, mentor, entrepreneur, and author of *Armor Your Mind*.

An active-duty military man and wellness professional, Carl has a unique perspective on what it takes to live a life of fulfillment. This resonates through his work, which focuses on nurturing mental resilience and emotional well-being no matter what challenges life brings.

Carl's work is informed by his struggles with confidence and outlook following a difficult childhood. These experiences feed into his extensive research and fuel his passion for helping others to overcome their obstacles to happiness. His willingness to draw on his personal experiences lends a warm and open quality to his work, making his style both engaging and informative.

With a firm belief in the power of positive thinking, Carl is adamant that his success in both his personal and professional life can be attributed to his positive outlook. A true believer in lifelong learning, he is currently pursuing professional certification in life coaching while continuing his mentor work, military service, and private business endeavors.

Carl strives to squeeze the most out of life at every opportunity, and this is clear in his passions and successes, which range from music and writing to business development and travel.

He lives in Texas with his beloved wife, Daria, and can often be found smoking a brisket or extracting the perfect cup of joe – to his mind, two of the greatest pleasures in life.

Made in United States
North Haven, CT
02 August 2022

22169149R00119